Collins

# Science Expert

## Biology 7

Series Editors
Meenakshi Atal
Manjuli Mukherjee

# Preface

***Collins Science Expert*** is a series of 14 coursebooks for Classes 1 to 8. The coursebooks for grades 1 and 2 are aligned with Environmental Studies (EVS) and grades 3 to 5 with Science. For Classes 6 to 8, there are separate coursebooks for Physics, Chemistry and Biology. This series, which is the revised edition of *Science Panorama*, is based on the **latest curriculum** prescribed by the **Council for the Indian School Certificate Examinations** and adheres to the guidelines of the *National Education Policy* (NEP) 2020.

In line with the curriculum, a thematic, coherent and structured approach has been followed and all new topics suggested in the curriculum have been included. The series also caters to the three domains of learning—**cognitive** (*intellectual nature*), **affective** (*attitudinal nature*) and **psychomotor** (*actionable nature*).

Aimed to answer a learner's cry: '*Teach me the way I want to learn*', this series adopts a method—**visual**, **auditory**, **kinesthetic** and **tactile** (**VAKT**)—that caters to all kinds of learners. Keeping in mind the saying 'I hear – I forget, I see – I understand and I do – I remember', a lot of hands-on activities have been incorporated. This would enable learners to understand and learn scientific concepts through experiential learning.

This series also emphasizes on developing *scientific skills* such as **observation**, **data collection**, **investigation**, **estimation**, **prediction**, **analysis** and **drawing inferences**. This would help in developing a scientific temperament in learners from a young age. The series also draws a connection between cause and effect; and focuses on the application of concepts in real-life situations. The language used is child-friendly and age-appropriate. Sufficient examples from everyday life have been given to help learners understand the concepts. A lot of colourful illustrations and well-labelled diagrams have been included to engage learners and aid in their understanding.

We would like to take this opportunity to thank all the teachers who reviewed the books and provided their valuable feedback, which helped in improving the quality of the content.

Any suggestions or constructive criticism from the users are welcome. We shall try to incorporate those in the future editions.

Authors

# Key Features

The key features of ***Collins Science Expert*** series are completely aligned with *National Education Policy* (NEP) 2020. These meticulously designed key features, based on VAKT (visual, auditory, kinesthetic and tactile) learning style and the three domains of Bloom's Taxonomy which include **cognitive (intellectual skills)**, **affective (attitudinal nature)** and **psychomotor (actionable nature)**, can be used as learning strategies to help in the development of scientific and 21st Century Skills in students. These key features also aim to help students shift from rote-learning to competency-based learning.

## Bloom's Taxonomy

### Cognitive Domain

- Focuses on intellectual skills such as critical thinking, problem solving, and creating a knowledge base
- Expects learners to progress linearly, beginning at "remember" and ending at "create."

- Prior Knowledge
- Learning Objectives
- Let's Get Started
- Quick Revision
- Talk Time
- Concept Map
- Keywords
- Exercise
- Word to know
- Review Corner

### Affective Domain

- Focuses on the attitudes, values, interests and appreciation of learners
- Focuses on allowing learners to understand what their own values are and how they have developed

- Greenathon
- Skill Booster
- Worksheets
- My Environment, My Responsibility!
- Happy Accidents
- Innovation: The Steppingstone
- Role of Science in Benefitting the Society

### Psycho motor Domain

- Encompasses the ability of learners to physically accomplish tasks and perform movement and skills
- Expects learners to progress from using reflexes and basic movement to non-discursive communication and meaningfully expressive activity

- Do It Yourself
- Activities
- Skill Booster
- Worksheets
- Innovation: The Steppingstone
- STEAM Worksheets

# Skills and Learnings

**Colour-coded tags and icons are used to easily identify the types of skills and learnings being addressed.**

**NEP Aligned Skills**

**21st Century Skills (21CS)**

**Learning Skills**
- Critical Thinking
- Creativity and Innovation
- Collaboration
- Communication

**Life Skills**
- Flexibility and Adaptability
- Leadership and Responsibility
- Initiative and Self-direction
- Productivity and Accountability
- Social and Cross-cultural Interaction

**Literacy Skills**
- Information Literacy
- Media Literacy
- Technology Literacy

**Experiential Learning (EL)**

**Cross Curricular (CC)**

**Bloom's Taxonomy (BT)**

**Art Integration (AI)**

**India Focus (IF)**

**SEE Learning**

# About the Features

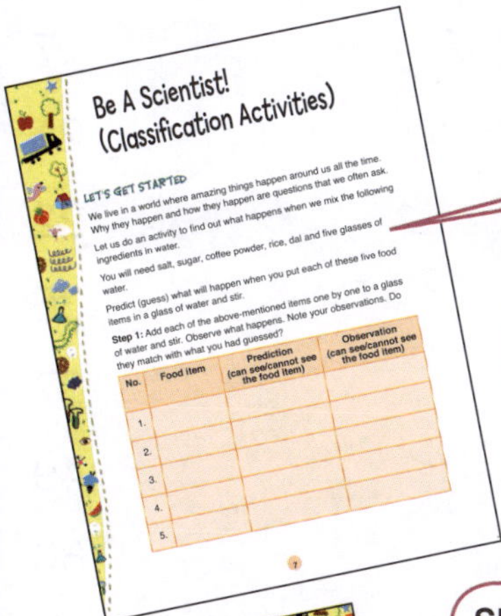


**Be a Scientist! (Classes 3 to 5):** Introduction to science process skills to help develop scientific attitudes

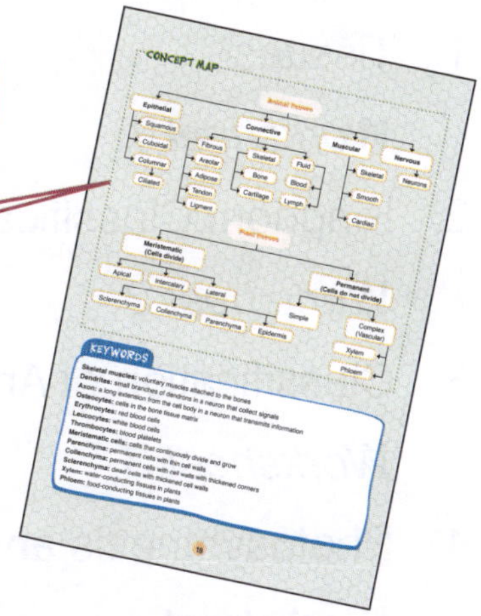


- **Concept Map:** Snapshot of the chapter in the form of a graphic organizer for quick recapitulation
- **Keywords:** Definitions of important terms

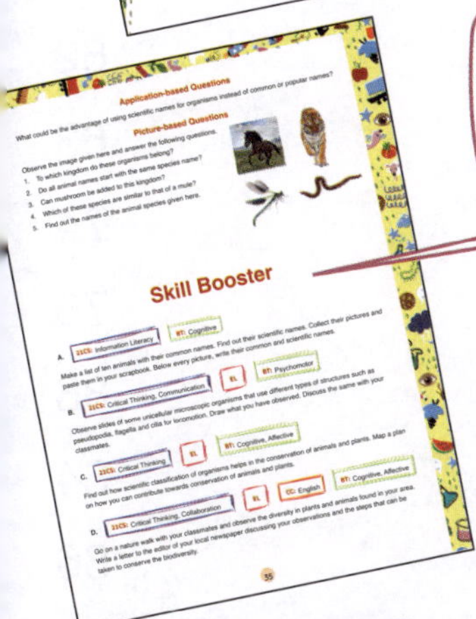


**Skill Booster:** Section aimed at imparting 21st Century Skills alongwith a focus on Cross-curricular Links, India Focus, Art Integration, Experiential Learning and Bloom's Taxonomy

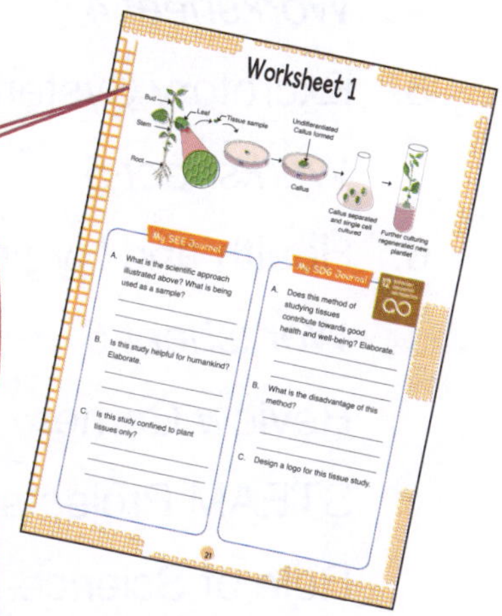


**Worksheet:** Interesting questions imparting skills catering to social, emotional and ethical (SEE) needs and United Nations' sustainable development goals (SDGs)

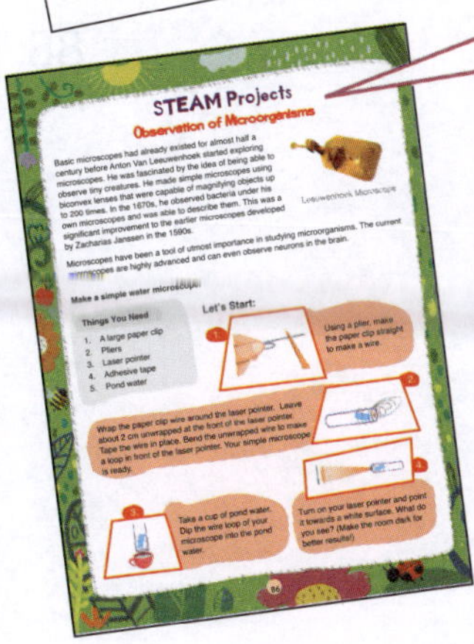


**My Environment, My Responsibility! (Classes 1 and 2):** Special pages to spread awareness and a sense of responsibility towards the environment

**Happy Accidents (Classes 3 to 8):** Interesting snippets on discoveries and inventions by chance/accidents that led to beneficial ways

**STEAM Worksheets (Physics 6 to 8):** Interesting project Ideas integrating Science, Technology, Engineering, Arts and Mathematics to solve real-world problems

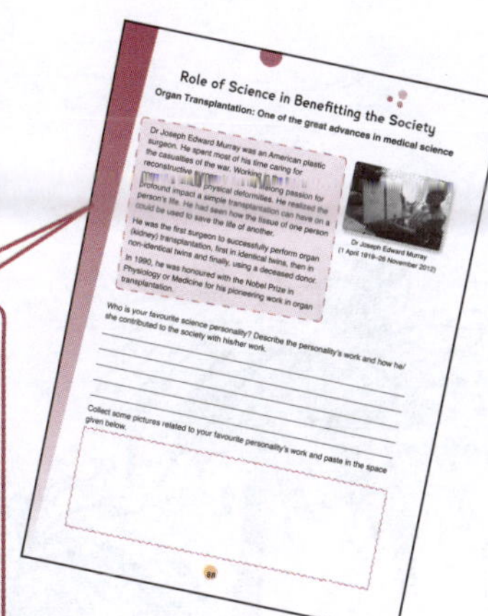


**My Eco Craft (Classes 1 and 2):** Hands-on activities to enhance learning beyond the classroom

**Innovation: The Steppingstone (Classes 3 to 5):** Ideas to guide students to solve real-life problems in innovative ways

**Role of Science in Benefitting the Society (Classes 6 to 8):** Snippets on the contributions made by various scientists for the development of the society

**Find Out:** Research-oriented questions requiring learners to look beyond the textbook

What do we call the person who treats our pet dog when it falls sick? FIND OUT

# Contents

# 1 Tissues

## Prior Knowledge

- Cells
- Structure of a cell
- Functions of cells
- Types and size of cells

## Learning Objectives

- Animal tissues
  - Epithelial tissue
  - Muscular tissue
  - Nervous tissue
  - Connective tissue
- Plant tissues
  - Meristematic tissue
  - Permanent tissue
    - Simple permanent tissue
    - Complex permanent tissue

## LET'S GET STARTED

Observe the image of different cells given here. Draw lines to match the images to the correct names.

1
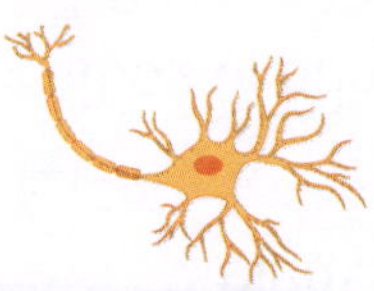
2
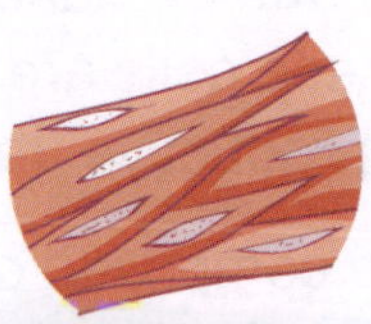
3
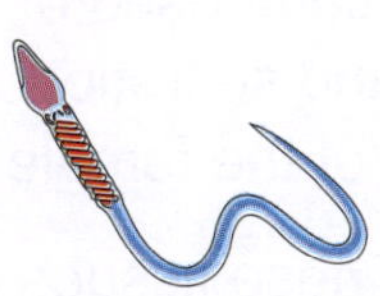
4

5
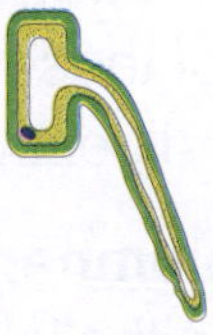
6
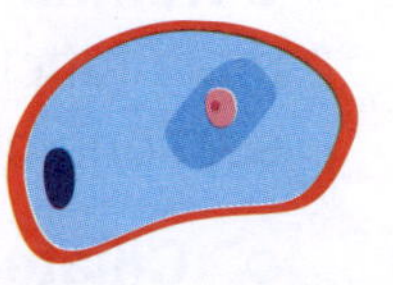

| a. Sperm cell | b. Smooth muscle cell | c. Plant root hair cell | d. Nerve cell | e. Pollen cell | f. Leaf cell |
|---|---|---|---|---|---|

In all multicellular organisms, groups of cells specialized to perform a common function form **tissues**. For example, in animals, muscle cells that have the ability to contract and relax form the muscular tissue, and nerve cells that have the ability to conduct messages to and from the brain form the nervous tissue. In plants, the cells of a bark form one type of tissue and the chlorophyll-containing cells in the leaf form another type of tissue.

In this chapter, we will learn about various plant and animal tissues, organs and organ systems.

## ANIMAL TISSUES

Animal tissues can be grouped into four basic types: epithelial tissues, muscular tissues, nervous tissues and connective tissues.

### Epithelial Tissues

- Epithelial tissues cover the entire internal and external surface of the body.
- They perform functions such as protection, absorption, secretion and sensory perception.
- The cells are found in layers, and there is little or no space between adjacent cells.
- The nucleus is present towards the base of the cells.
- All epithelial tissues are separated from the other tissues with a thin layer of connecting tissue called the **basement membrane**.
- The basement membrane provides structural support while binding to the neighbouring structures.

Depending on the specific function and the shape and size of the cells, epithelial tissues can be grouped into the following types (Fig. 1.1):

- **Squamous epithelium:** These tissues are composed of flattened and thin cells. The main function of these cells is to provide a smooth and protective surface. These cells are found in the alveoli of lungs, segments of kidney tubules and the lining of capillaries.
- **Cuboidal epithelium:** These tissues are composed of box-like cells. The main function of these cells is secretion and absorption. These cells are found in the lining of the kidney tubules and in the ducts of glands.
- **Columnar epithelium:** These tissues are composed of tall and cylindrical cells. The main function of these cells is absorption and secretion. These cells are found in some sections of the digestive system and parts of the female reproductive tract.
    - **Ciliated columnar epithelial tissue:** These tissues are composed of simple columnar epithelial cells with cilia on their apical surfaces. The main function of these cells is movement of substances. These cells are found in the lining of the fallopian tubes and parts of the respiratory system.

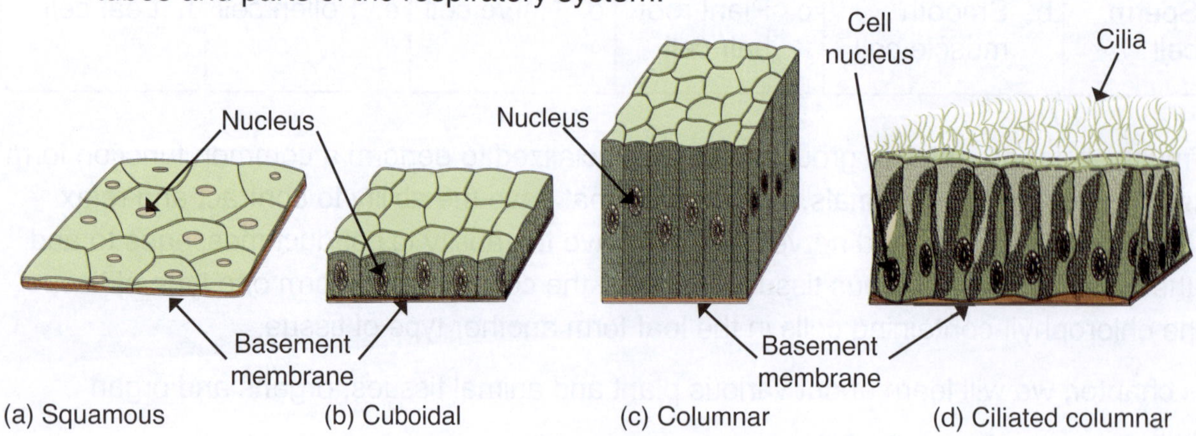


*Fig. 1.1 Epithelial tissue*

## Muscular Tissues

Muscular tissues are present in the muscles of the body. Muscles contract and relax to bring about movement of body parts in animals. They also provide mechanical support. The human body is made up of more than 600 muscles.

Depending upon the structure and function, muscles can be grouped into three basic types (Fig. 1.2): skeletal muscles, smooth muscles and cardiac muscles.

### *Skeletal Muscles*

- These muscles are attached to the bones; hence, they are called skeletal muscles. They help in the movement of bones.
- The skeletal muscles are long and cylindrical. They have many nuclei (plural of nucleus).
- Alternate dark and light bands are present that give these muscles a striated appearance. Therefore, they are also called **striated muscles**.
- These muscles are voluntary in action, that is, we can control their movement. That is why, these muscles are also known as **voluntary muscles**. For example, we can bend our arm with the help of the striated muscles in our arm.

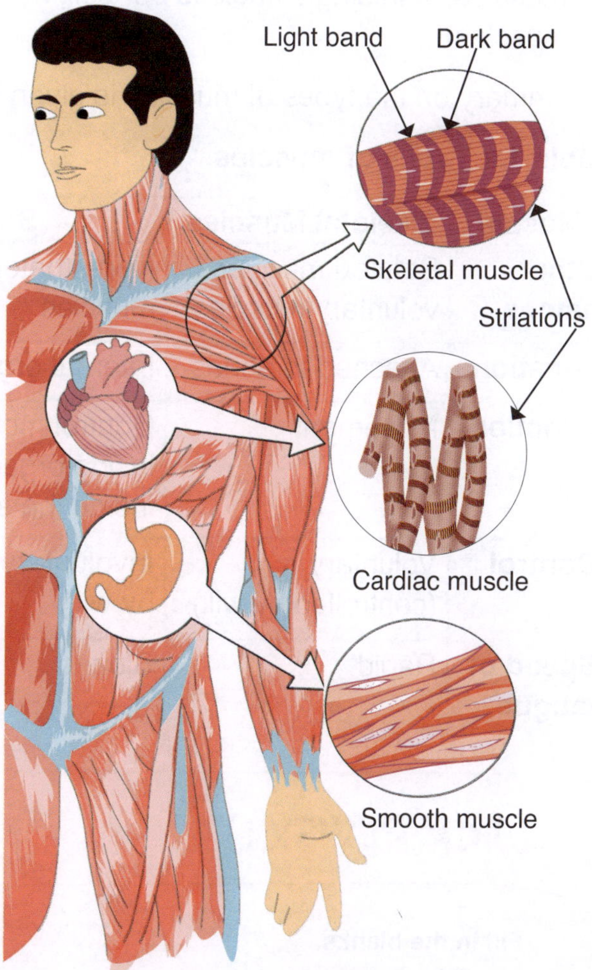

*Fig. 1.2 Types of muscular tissues*

### *Smooth Muscles*

- The smooth muscles are spindle-shaped (thin and elongated) with a single large oval-shaped nucleus.
- These muscles do not have bands or striation, and hence the name **smooth muscles**.
- Smooth muscles are found in the inner layers of the digestive tract, the urinary bladder, the uterus and the blood vessels.
- All smooth muscles are involuntary. We cannot control the muscles of our stomach or blood vessels. That is why these muscles are also known as **involuntary muscles**.

> **FIND OUT**
> Which are the largest and the smallest muscles in the body?

## Cardiac Muscles

- Muscles specifically found in the walls of the heart are called cardiac muscles.
- They are special muscles that work non-stop without getting tired.
- Structurally, cardiac muscles are short, branched, cross-striated muscles (like skeletal muscles) with single nucleus per cell, but functionally, they are involuntary (like smooth muscles).

A summary on the types of muscles is given in Table 1.1.

**Table 1.1 Types of muscles**

| Muscle | Skeletal Muscles | Smooth Muscles | Cardiac Muscles |
|---|---|---|---|
| **Other names** | Striated muscles, voluntary muscles | Non-striated muscles, involuntary muscles | Heart muscles |
| **Location** | Attached to bones | Internal organs such as stomach | Heart |
| **Function** | Movement | Control movement of substances inside organs. For example, food inside the stomach. | Beating of the heart |
| **Control** | Voluntary (controlled by will) | Involuntary (cannot be controlled by will) | Involuntary |
| **Speed of fatigue** | Rapid | Slow | Do not get fatigued during the lifetime of an organism |

## QUICK REVISION

**Fill in the blanks.**

1. ________ (Epithelial/Muscular) tissues cover the entire internal and external surfaces of the body.
2. ________ (Skeletal/Cardiac) muscles work non-stop without getting tired.
3. Smooth muscles are ________ (voluntary/involuntary).
4. ________ (Skeletal/Smooth) muscles are attached to bones.

## Nervous Tissues

Nervous tissues are made up of nerve cells called **neurons** (Fig. 1.3). Neurons are grouped together in the form of bundles called **nerves**. Nerves run throughout the body forming a network.

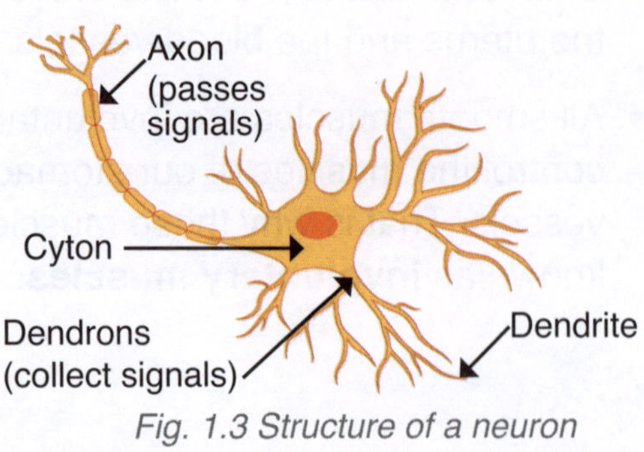

*Fig. 1.3 Structure of a neuron*

Structurally, a neuron consists of the following parts.

- **Cyton:** the cell body
- **Dendrons:** finger-like projections extending from the cell body
- **Dendrites:** branches of dendrons
- **Axon:** the longest extension from the cell body

**TALK TIME**
How is the nervous system programmed to function?

## Connective Tissues

These tissues are found in the body in abundance. Their basic function is to bind one type of tissue with the other and to support organs and hold them in place. Connective tissues are made up of a matrix and a ground substance. The matrix consists of living cells and the ground substance consists of non-living substances such as proteins and minerals.

Connective tissues can be grouped into three categories: fibrous tissues, skeletal tissues and fluid tissues.

### *Fibrous Tissues*

Fibrous tissues pack and bind organs. These tissues can be further grouped into the following types.

**Areolar tissues**

- These tissues have a jelly-like matrix that encloses different kinds of cells [Fig. 1.4(a)].
- The matrix helps bind skin to muscles, fill gaps between cells and holds organs in place. It has elastic fibres.
- These are found in the linings of the gut, muscles, skin and other organs.

**Adipose tissues**

- These tissues are connective tissues that surround the organs.
- They are also found beneath the skin and act as a cushion and insulator in the body.
- They are also called **body fat** as they store energy in the form of fat [Fig. 1.4(b)].

**Tendons**

- Tendons are whitish, tough cords of thick, fibrous tissues that connect muscles to bones [Fig. 1.4(c)].

**Ligaments**

- Ligaments are bands of elastic fibres that connect different bones [Fig. 1.4(c)].

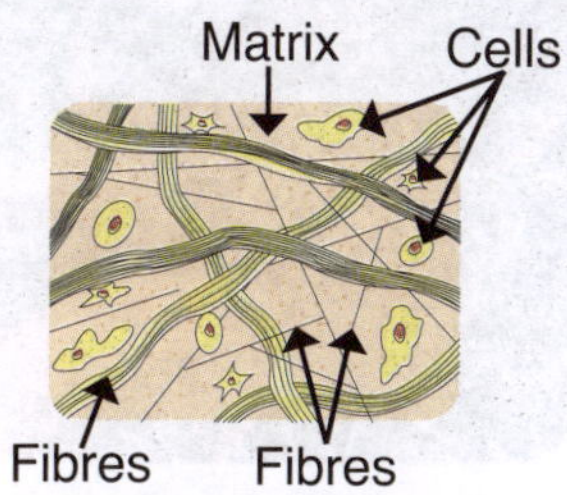

(a) Areolar tissue

(b) Adipose tissue

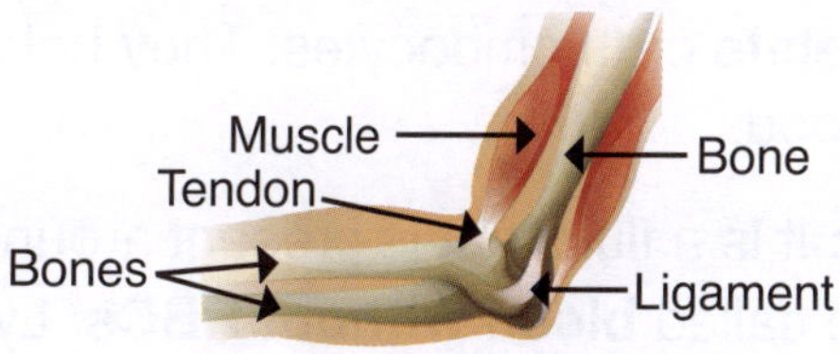

(c) Tendon and ligament

*Fig. 1.4 Fibrous connective tissues*

## *Skeletal Tissues*

Skeletal connective tissues provide a supportive framework to the body and can be further grouped into two types: bone and cartilage.

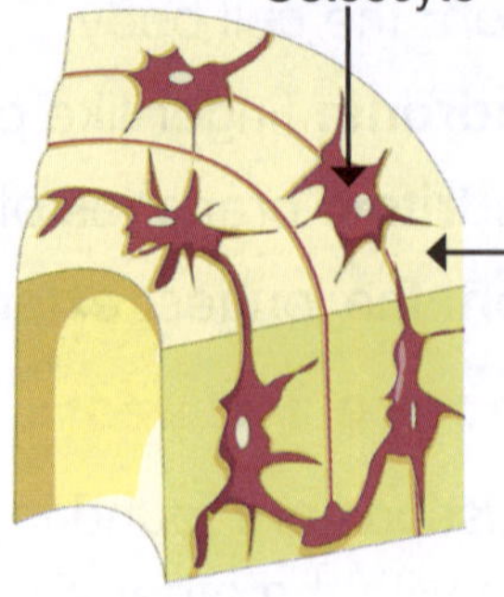


Fig. 1.5 Bone tissue

### Bone

- It is the hardest and the most rigid connective tissue. It consists of living cells, called **osteocytes**, which are enclosed in the bone matrix (Fig. 1.5).
- It is made of calcium and phosphate along with traces of sodium and magnesium.

### Cartilage

- It is a flexible, elastic, semi-transparent but tough connective tissue.
- It is usually found at the end of the bones, where it reduces friction between two bones, and in the walls of the windpipe, the tip of the nose and the pinna of the ear.
- The cartilage cells, called **chondrocytes**, are scattered in the matrix (chondroitin) (Fig. 1.6).

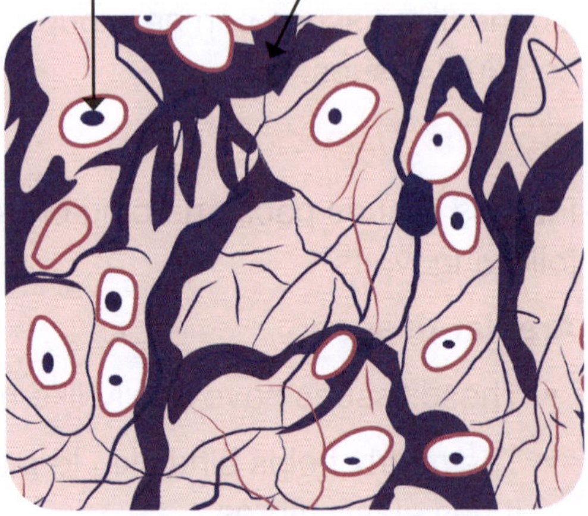


Fig. 1.6 Cartilage tissue

## *Fluid Connective Tissues*

Fluid connective tissues help in the transportation of nutrients and essential substances within the body.

They can be further grouped into two types: blood and lymph.

**DO YOU KNOW?**

A shark's skeleton is made entirely of cartilage!

**Blood:** It consists of **plasma** (the watery matrix) in which three types of cells (Fig. 1.7) are found.

- **Red blood cells** (RBCs) or erythrocytes: They transport oxygen and carbon dioxide in the body.
- **White blood cells** (WBCs) or leucocytes: They help the body fight against pathogens and other foreign substances.
- **Platelets** or thrombocytes: They help in clotting of blood.

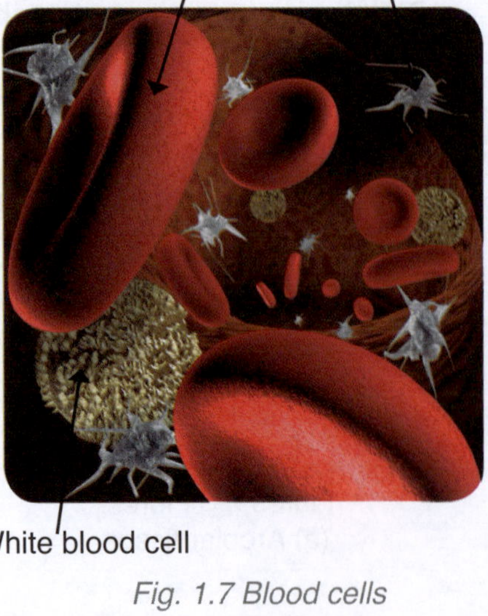


Fig. 1.7 Blood cells

**Lymph:** It is a fluid that is present around body cells. It is also called **blood without RBCs**. Lymph fluids protect the body against any infection.

## ACTIVITY 1

**Aim:** To observe the slides of animal tissues

**Materials required:** Permanent slides of animal tissues and microscope

**Procedure:**

1. Ask your teacher to provide some permanent slides of animal tissues.
2. Focus these slides under a microscope with your teacher's help and observe.

**Observation:** Draw what you see in your notebook and write two characteristics of each tissue.

## QUICK REVISION

**Match the following.**

| | |
|---|---|
| 1. Adipose tissue | a. Connects muscle to bone |
| 2. Tendon | b. Stores fat |
| 3. Fluid connective tissue | c. Neuron |
| 4. Nervous tissue | d. Lymph |

## PLANT TISSUES

Plant tissues can be divided into two categories: meristematic tissues and permanent tissues (Fig. 1.8).

### Meristematic Tissues

- Cells of the meristematic tissues are small and thin-walled with large nuclei and almost no vacuoles and intercellular space. These cells divide actively giving rise to more cells.
- Meristematic tissues help in growth.

Meristematic tissues are of three types: apical, intercalary and lateral.

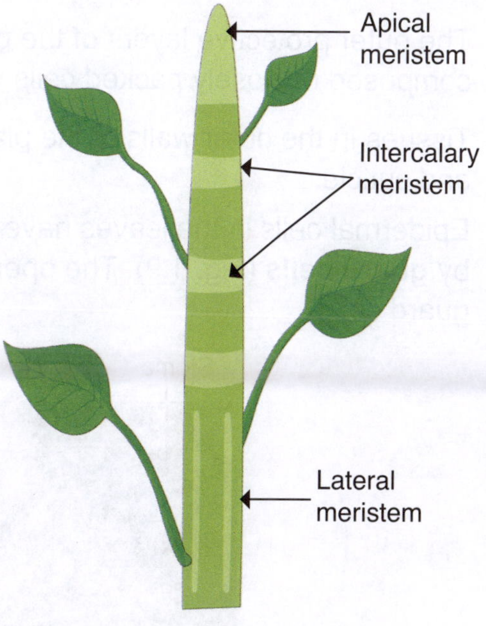

*Fig. 1.8 Meristematic tissues*

**Apical meristem:** It is present at the tip of the growing parts such as the tip of the root, stem and branches. It causes growth at the root and shoot tips.

**Intercalary meristem:** It is found in places where the stem is attached with the leaves and at the base of the leaves. It causes an increase in the length of the stem.

**Lateral meristem:** It is present between water-conducting and food-conducting tissues. It causes an increase in the thickness of the stem.

A summary on the types of meristematic tissue is given in Table 1.2.

**Table 1.2 Types of meristematic tissues**

| Type | Location | Function |
|---|---|---|
| Apical meristem | Root and shoot tips | Growth |
| Intercalary meristem | Base of leaves and place of attachment of stem and leaves | Increases length of the stem |
| Lateral meristem | Between water-conducting and food-conducting tissues | Increases thickness of the stem |

## Permanent Tissues

These tissues form the bulk of the plant body. The cells do not grow or divide after reaching a certain size. Permanent tissues are of two types: simple permanent tissues and complex permanent tissues.

### *Simple Permanent Tissues*

Based on their functions, simple permanent tissues can be grouped into two types: protective tissues and supporting tissues.

#### *Protective Tissues*

- The outer protective layers of the plant are commonly known as **epidermis**. They are composed of closely packed cells without intercellular spaces.
- Tissues in the outer walls of the plant are usually thickened and covered with wax and cuticle.
- Epidermal cells in the leaves have openings called **stomata**, which are surrounded by **guard cells** (Fig. 1.9). The opening and closing of stomata are regulated by the guard cells.

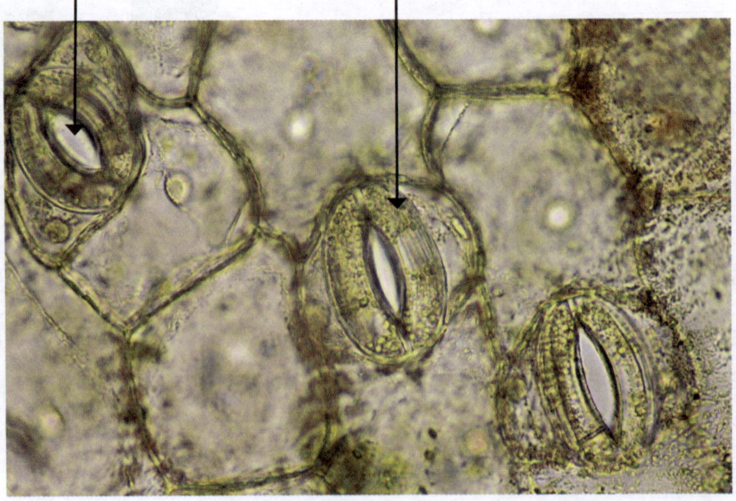


*Fig. 1.9 Epidermis*

## *Supporting Tissues*

These tissues constitute the primary plant body or the bulk of the plant. These tissues can be further grouped into three types: parenchyma, collenchyma and sclerenchyma.

- **Parenchyma:** These tissues are found in all soft parts of the plant. Cells are round to oval in shape with thin, flexible cell walls and a large vacuole with an ample intercellular space [Fig. 1.10(a)]. These cells help in the storage of food and water. The intercellular space aids in the exchange of gases in the cells of the plant.
- **Collenchyma:** These tissues have elongated cells that are thicker at the corners and are made of substances called **cellulose** and **pectin**. They are found under the epidermis of the plant. These cells may sometimes contain chloroplasts [Fig. 1.10(b)]. These cells provide structural support and elasticity to the stem and leaves of the plant.
- **Sclerenchyma:** These tissues are dead cells with a very thick cell wall made of cellulose and lignin. They are found in the veins and stems of the plant [Fig. 1.10(c)]. The function of sclerenchyma cells is to provide support and rigidity.

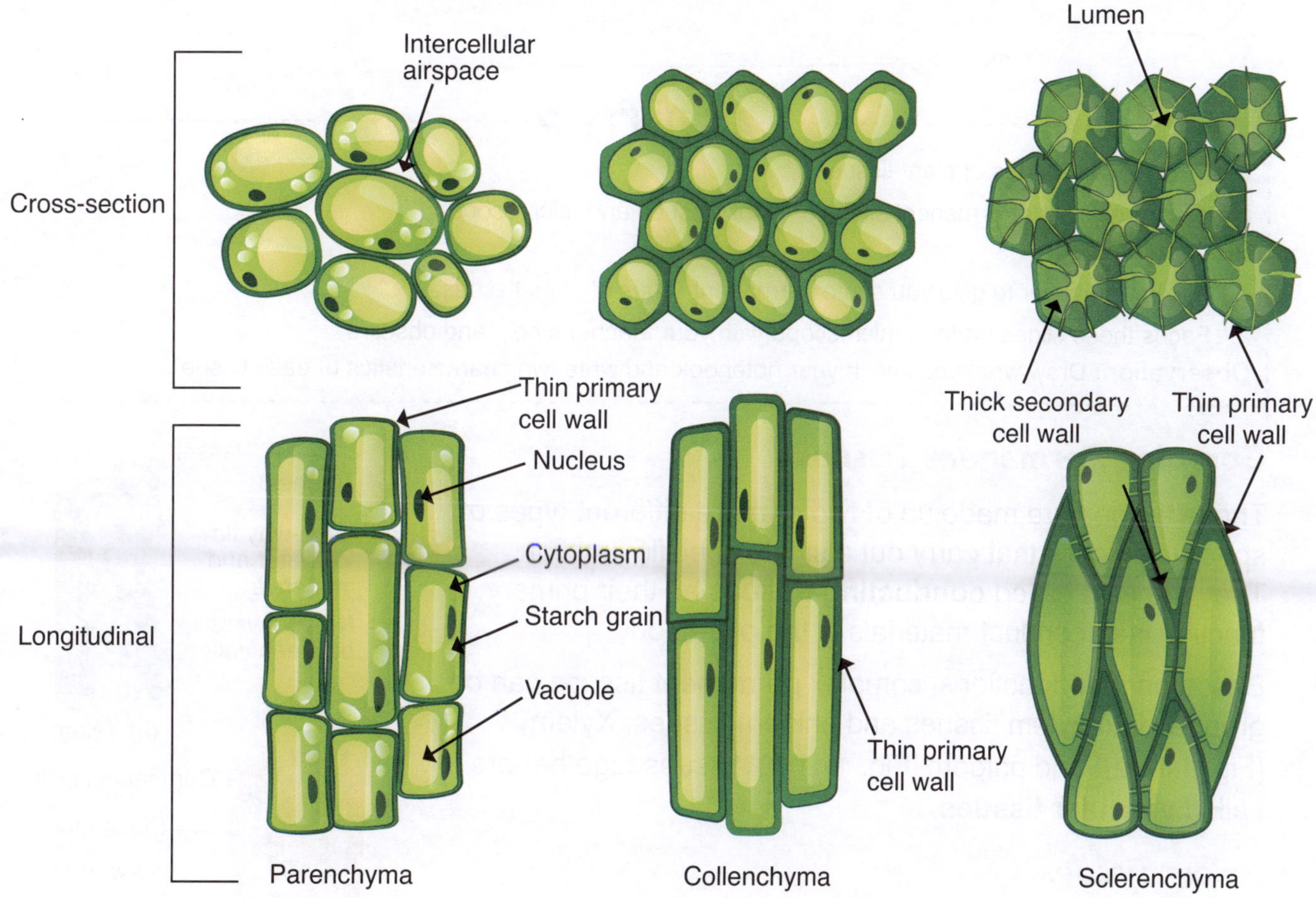


*Fig. 1.10 Supporting tissues*

**DO YOU KNOW?**

Celery is crunchy because it is made of collenchyma tissues filled with water. The pressure of the water against the cell walls creates a stiffness, giving it a crunch.

## QUICK REVISION

**Complete the table.**

| Category | Parenchyma | Collenchyma | Sclerenchyma |
|---|---|---|---|
| **Location** | Stem, root, leaves, flowers, widely distributed in fruits | | |
| **Shape of cells** | | Cells are living; circular, oval or polygonal with thickened corners of walls | Cells are dead; long, narrow, pointed; uniformly thick walls |
| **Arrangement of cells** | Loosely arranged with intercellular spaces | | Intercellular spaces absent |
| **Functions** | Stores and assimilates food; provides mechanical support; stores waste products such as tannin, gum and resins | | |

## ACTIVITY 2

**Aim:** To view the slides of plant tissues

**Materials required:** Permanent slides of plant tissues and microscope

**Procedure:**

1. Ask your teacher to give you some permanent slides of plant tissues.
2. Focus these slides under a microscope with your teacher's help and observe.

**Observation:** Draw what you see in your notebook and write two characteristics of each tissue.

## *Complex Permanent Tissues*

These tissues are made up of two or more different types of specialized cells that carry out a single specific function. They are also called **conducting tissues** as their primary function is to conduct materials in the plant body.

Based on their functions, complex permanent tissues can be grouped into xylem tissues and phloem tissues. Xylem [Fig. 1.11(a)] and phloem [Fig. 1.11(b)] tissues together are called **vascular tissues**.

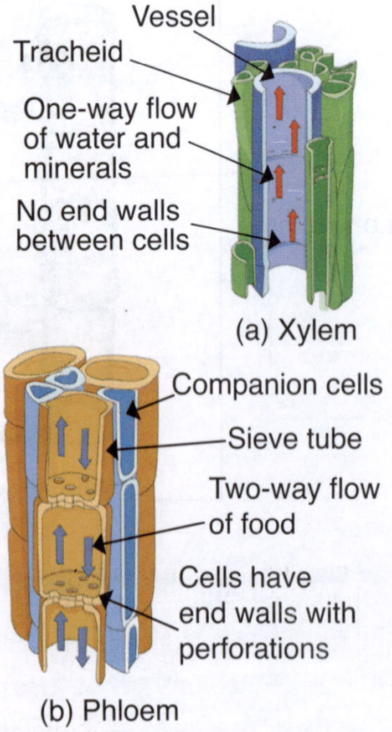

*Fig. 1.11 Complex permanent tissues*

### *Xylem Tissues*

- Xylem is a bundle of cells that are often dead.
- They have thick cell walls and are placed end to end, one above the other to form a pipeline.
- Xylem is composed of different types of cells called vessels and tracheids. It also contains fibres and parenchyma.
- The function of xylem tissues is to transport water and minerals from the roots to the other parts of the plant.

### *Phloem Tissues*

- Phloem is a bundle of living cells with narrow, elongated and thin cell walls.
- Phloem is composed of sieve tubes and companion cells. It also contains fibres and parenchyma.
- Main functions of phloem tissues include transportation of food prepared in the leaves to various plant parts.

## ACTIVITY 3

**Aim:** To observe the stomata in a leaf of a balsam plant

**Materials required:** Fresh balsam leaf, distilled water, glycerine, safranin stain, glass plate, slide, coverslip and microscope

**Procedure:**

1. Take a fresh balsam leaf, fold it carefully and tear along the lower side of the leaf.
2. A colourless narrow border (epidermis) found along the torn edge should be carefully pulled out.
3. Place the epidermis in a glass plate containing distilled water.
4. Transfer the epidermis onto a glass slide and add a drop of safranin solution. Leave it for 30–60 seconds to stain the peel.
5. Remove excess stain by rinsing it with distilled water.
6. Add a few drops of glycerine and cover it with a coverslip.

**Observation:** Draw what you see in your notebook. Compare this with the diagram of the epidermis and stomata given in the earlier sections of the chapter.

## ACTIVITY 4

**Aim**: To infer that transportation of water and minerals takes place through xylem

**Materials required:** Glass beaker, water, a plant twig, stain/ink, coverslip, blade, slide and microscope

**Procedure:**

1. Fill about three-fourths of a glass beaker with water.
2. Place a plant twig in the beaker.
3. Add a few drops of ink to the beaker and leave it for some time.
4. Cut a thin section of the plant stem from the set-up with the help of a blade.
5. Transfer the section to a clean glass slide.
6. Place a coverslip and focus the slide under the microscope with the help of your teacher.

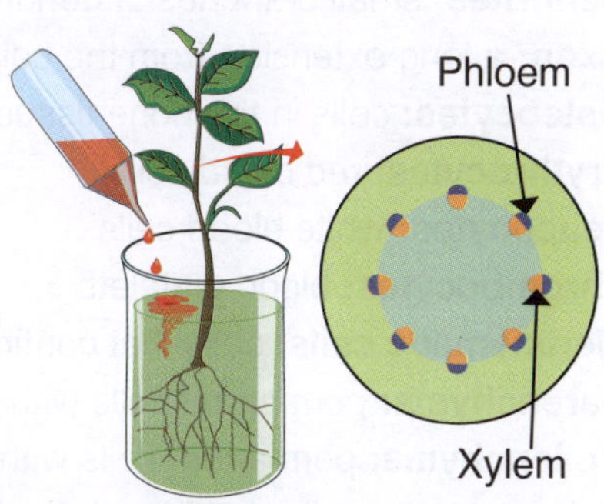


**Observation**: Tubes coloured with the colour of the ink are visible towards the centre of the section.

**Conclusion:** Water is transported from the roots to other parts of the plant body through xylem, and when a section of the stem is viewed under the microscope, a few parts of the tissues in the vascular bundles appear coloured. These are the xylem tissues.

## CONCEPT MAP

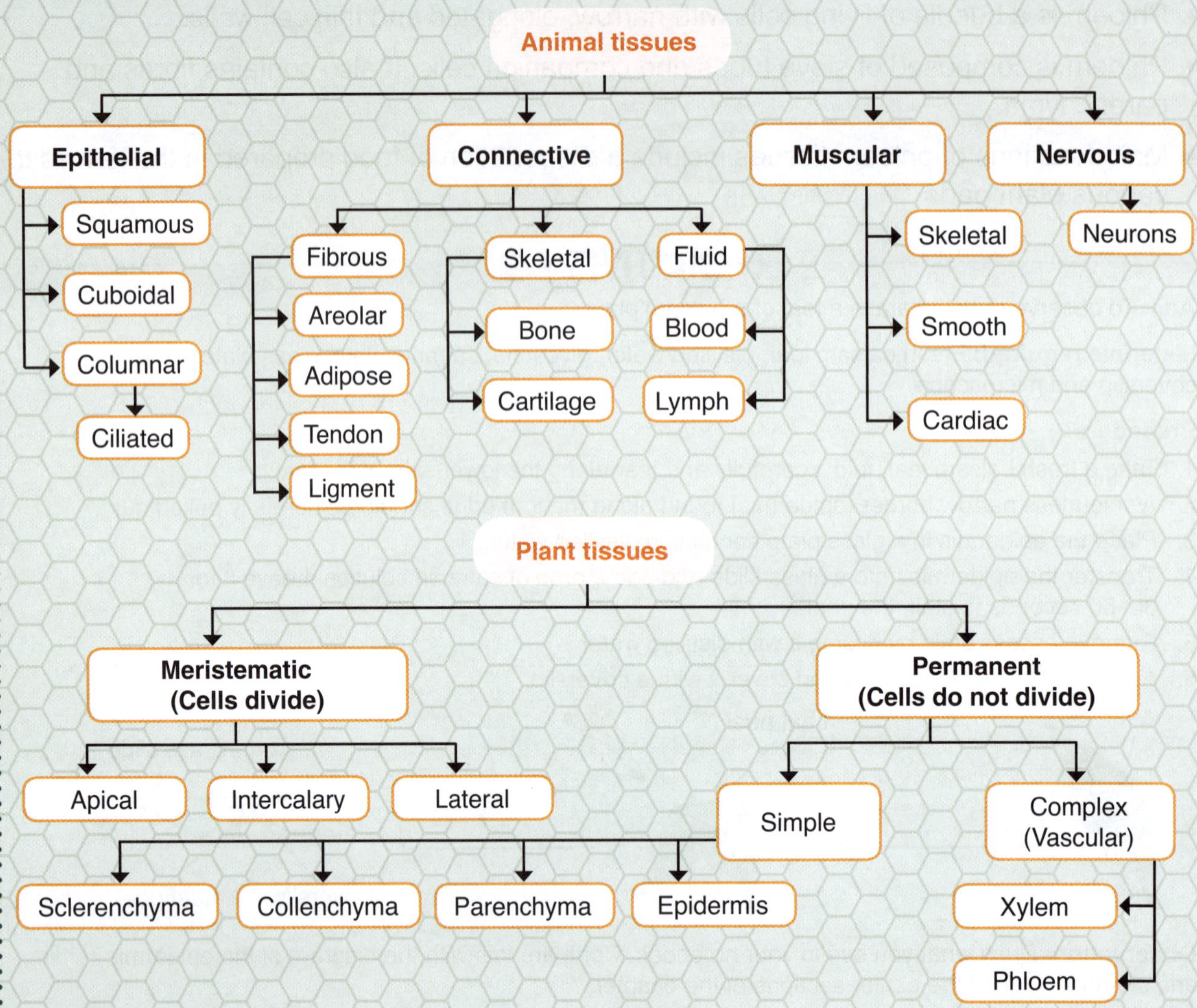


## KEYWORDS

**Skeletal muscles:** voluntary muscles attached to the bones
**Dendrites:** small branches of dendrons in a neuron that collect signals
**Axon:** a long extension from the cell body in a neuron that transmits information
**Osteocytes:** cells in the bone tissue matrix
**Erythrocytes:** red blood cells
**Leucocytes:** white blood cells
**Thrombocytes:** blood platelets
**Meristematic cells:** cells that continuously divide and grow
**Parenchyma:** permanent cells with thin cell walls
**Collenchyma:** permanent cells with cell walls with thickened corners
**Sclerenchyma:** dead cells with thickened cell walls
**Xylem:** water-conducting tissues in plants
**Phloem:** food-conducting tissues in plants

# Exercise

## Objective Type Questions

**A. Choose the correct answer.**

1. Which of the following tissues are found in the lining of blood vessels?
   a. Muscular  b. Nervous
   c. Epithelial  d. Connective
2. Tendon connects the __________.
   a. ligament to bone
   b. bone to bone
   c. muscle to bone
   d. muscle to ligament
3. Neurons are cells of the __________ system.
   a. digestive  b. skeletal
   c. respiratory  d. nervous
4. Adipose tissues store __________.
   a. fats  b. carbohydrates
   c. proteins  d. vitamins
5. Which of the following plant tissues conducts food?
   a. Parenchyma  b. Phloem
   c. Collenchyma  d. Xylem

**B. Fill in the blanks.**

1. Areolar connective tissue has a __________ (fluid/fibrous) matrix.
2. Lymph is blood without __________ (white/red) blood cells.
3. Chondrocytes are cells of the __________ (bones/cartilage).
4. Lateral meristem causes growth in __________ (length/thickness).
5. Sieve tubes are found in __________ (xylem/phloem) tissues.

**C. Write T for True and F for False.**

1. Cells of epithelial tissues have a basement membrane.
2. Smooth muscles are striated and can be controlled by will.
3. Cartilage is a connective tissue usually found at the end of the bones.
4. Parenchyma is a type of simple permanent tissue.
5. Sclerenchyma has elongated cells that are thick at the corners.

**D. Arrange the words in a proper sequence.**

1. epithelium/composed/flattened/of/and/thin/are/cells/Squamous
2. In/muscle/help/movement/tissue
3. carbon dioxide/the/oxygen/transport/body/RBCs/and/in
4. Maintain/connective/tissues/interconnection/different/between/different/organs.
5. Specialized/permanent/tissues/are/tissues/multiply/not/actively/do/that

## Subjective Type Questions

**A. Define the following.**

1. Tissues
2. Columnar epithelial tissues
3. Ligaments
4. Fluid connective tissues
5. Apical tissues

**B. Differentiate between the following.**

1. Skeletal muscles and smooth muscles
2. Ligament and tendon
3. Areolar tissues and adipose tissues
4. Meristematic and permanent tissues
5. Xylem and phloem

**C. Answer the following questions in brief.**

1. What are the three types of epithelial tissues?
2. What are tendons and ligaments?
3. What are osteocytes?
4. Which tissue causes growth in plants?
5. What is epidermis in plants?

**D. Answer the following questions in detail.**

1. Write a note on epithelial tissues.
2. What are muscular tissues? Explain the three types of muscular tissues.
3. Write a note on fibrous connective tissue.
4. Write a short note on fluid connective tissues.
5. Describe the vascular tissues found in plants.

## Application-based Question

An individual who had broken his arm is suggested to take rest and not move his arm. What will happen if the broken arm is let to move freely?

## Picture-based Questions

Observe the image and answer the following questions.

1. Identify and name the types of tissues shown here.
2. Label the diagrams.
3. What are the functions of these tissues?
4. What is the main difference between these tissues?
5. Where are these tissues found?

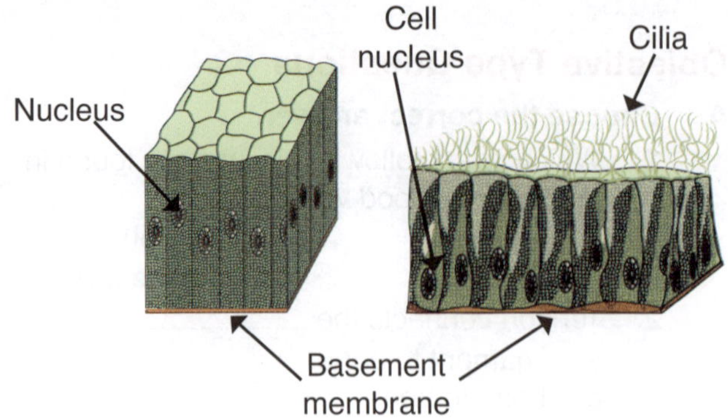


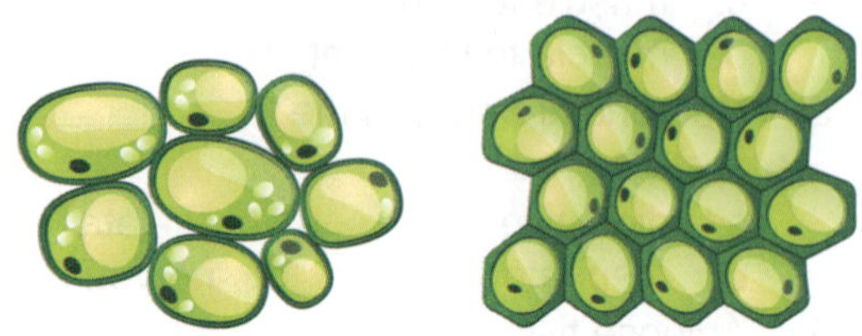

# Skill Booster

**A.** **21CS:** Information Literacy | **CC:** Computer Science | **BT:** Cognitive

Find out how many different layers are there in the human integumentary system. Prepare a presentation based on your findings.

**B.** **21CS:** Technology Literacy | **CC:** English | **BT:** Cognitive, Affective

With advancements in technology, scientists have been able to generate tissues under artificial conditions in laboratories. This technique is called tissue culture.

Find out more about the process and its merits and demerits. Write a report based on your findings.

**C.** **21CS:** Critical Thinking | **EL** | **BT:** Psychomotor

Do an activity to observe the conduction of water by the stem.

**Materials required:** Two long twigs of white chrysanthemum or white carnation with a flower on each, food dyes or ink, two beakers and water

**Procedure:**

1. Take equal volume of water in the beakers. Mark them as A and B.
2. Add ink to the water in beaker B. You can also add food dyes instead of ink.
3. Place one twig in each beaker and leave the set-up for 24 hours.

**Observation:** Observe the colour of the flower on each twig after 24 hours.

Discuss your observations in class. What do you infer from the observation?

# Worksheet 1

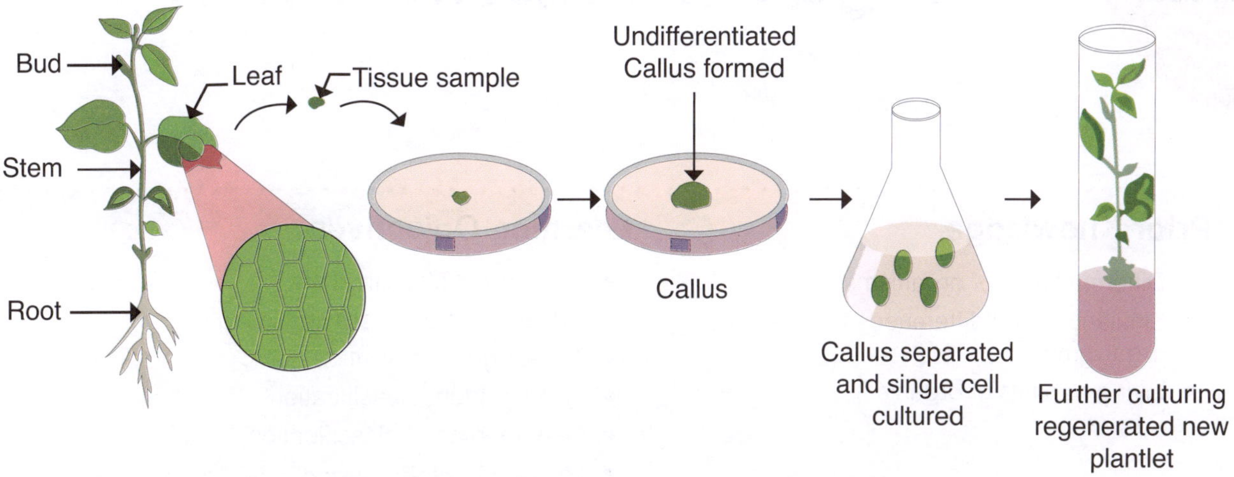


## My SEE Journal

A. What is the scientific approach illustrated above? What is being used as a sample?

______________________________

______________________________

______________________________

B. Is this study helpful for humankind? Elaborate.

______________________________

______________________________

______________________________

C. Is this study confined to plant tissues only?

______________________________

______________________________

______________________________

## My SDG Journal

12 RESPONSIBLE CONSUMPTION AND PRODUCTION

A. Does this method of studying tissues contribute towards good health and well-being? Elaborate.

______________________________

______________________________

______________________________

B. What is the disadvantage of this method?

______________________________

______________________________

______________________________

C. Design a logo for this tissue study.

# 2 Kingdom Classification

**Prior Knowledge**

- Different types of organisms
- Similarities and differences between the organisms
- Living habitats of organisms

**Learning Objectives**

- Meaning of classification
- Advantages of classifying living things
- Two-kingdom classification
- Five-kingdom classification
- General plan of classification
- More on bacteria, *Amoeba* and fungi

## LET'S GET STARTED

A list of animals is given in the chart. Read the parameters given in the chart and complete the table.

| | Animal | Lives in/on (Land/sea/air) | Type of Skin | Size (Bigger/smaller than an average adult human) | Kind of Babies (Giving birth/ laying eggs) |
|---|---|---|---|---|---|
| 1 | Cow | | | | |
| 2 | Fish | | | | |
| 3 | Bird | | | | |
| 4 | Dolphin | | | | |
| 5 | Horse | | | | |
| 6 | Frog | | | | |
| 7 | Bear | | | | |

The term **classification** means to sort or categorize things into groups. In our daily lives, we often come across situations where things have been sorted into groups. For example, in a supermarket, food items are sorted into various categories such as vegetables, fruits, spices and packaged foods.

There are around 30 million types of living organisms on Earth. It would be impossible to locate and study these without sorting them first into groups. Scientists realized this need a long time ago and started categorizing organisms under separate groups based on similar characteristics to make their study easier.

## BIOLOGICAL CLASSIFICATION

Classifying living organisms into different groups and subgroups based on similarities in their characteristics is called **biological classification**.

> **DO YOU KNOW?**
>
> **Taxonomy** is the branch of biology that systematically classifies living things based on similarities in structure, origin, etc. Scientists who study taxonomy are called **taxonomists**.

**The advantages of classifying living things are:**

- Classification makes it easy to identify and study living organisms on the Earth.
- Classification helps in identifying a new organism and placing it in a particular group.
- It helps in getting an overview of the characteristics of a particular group of organisms, so that one does not need to memorize the characteristics of each type of organism in that group.
- It gives a clear idea about the evolution of organisms from simple forms to more complex ones.
- It establishes the relationship between different living things.

## DIFFERENT SYSTEMS OF CLASSIFICATION

Living things are classified based on their habits, habitats, mode of reproduction and other features.

Aristotle, a Greek philosopher, was the first to classify animals based on simple visible characteristics such as the type of body covering (hard or soft), the mode of reproduction (laying eggs or giving birth to young ones) and the presence or absence of red-coloured blood.

Theophrastus, a follower and successor of Aristotle, classified plants on the basis of size into herbs, shrubs, undershrubs and trees.

The above-mentioned method of classification based on visible characteristics had some major drawbacks. Two very different organisms could be put in the same group; for example, based on the presence of wings, birds and insects can be categorized under the same group, although they are very different in other characteristics. Similarly, rose plants and ferns can be categorized under the same group based on size despite their differences.

### Two-Kingdom Classification

To overcome these drawbacks, in the year 1758, a Swedish botanist named Carolus Linnaeus proposed a more scientific method of classification. He classified living organisms into two kingdoms: Kingdom Plantae and Kingdom Animalia.

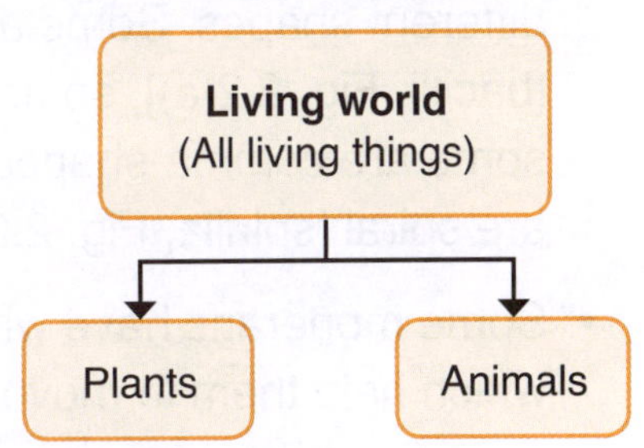


#### *Kingdom Plantae*

It includes organisms that prepare their own food but are stationary, that is they cannot move around.

#### *Kingdom Animalia*

It includes organisms that cannot prepare their own food but can move around.

Linnaeus further classified each kingdom into smaller groups based on similar characteristics. Each group was further divided into subgroups and so on. This way, several taxonomic ranks were developed. The lowest rank had organisms with most features in common, that is they were the most closely related.

## Five-Kingdom Classification

Microorganisms were discovered after the invention of the microscope. With advances in technology, powerful microscopes were built, which gave a better understanding of the cell structure of microorganisms. Microorganisms were found to have characteristics that made them unsuitable to be grouped under the plant or the animal kingdom. Further observations and discoveries led to an increased knowledge about the evolution and structures of organisms. As a result, the two-kingdom classification began to be considered inadequate to group all these organisms.

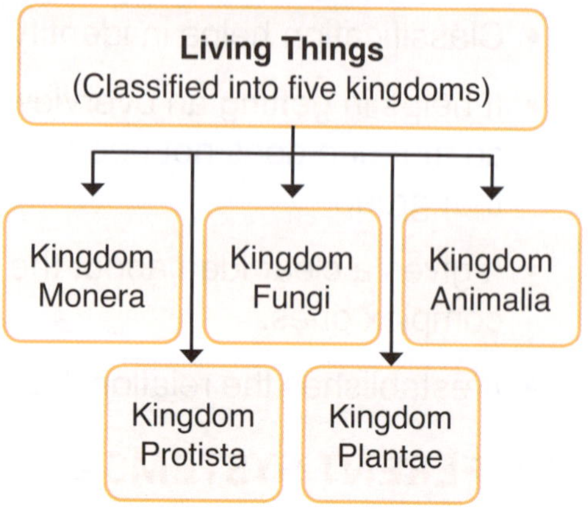


In 1969, RH Whittaker proposed the **five-kingdom classification** system to cater to the necessity of classifying all known organisms.

Let us look at the characteristics of the organisms grouped under each kingdom.

## Kingdom Monera

- They are unicellular, that is the entire body is made up of a single cell.
- The cells (Fig. 2.1) lack a well-defined nucleus. The genetic material in the cell lies in the cytoplasm.
- Their cells have a **cell wall** as an outer covering.
- Some organisms in this kingdom are **autotrophic**, that is they can prepare their own food, for example, blue–green algae, while others are **heterotrophic**, that is they depend on other sources for food, for example, *E. coli*.
- Bacteria are grouped under this kingdom and have different shapes. Some are long and rod-like [bacilli, Fig. 2.2(a)], some are spherical [cocci, Fig. 2.2(b)], some are comma-shaped [*Vibrio*, Fig. 2.2(c)] and some are spiral [spirilla, Fig. 2.2(d)].
- Some monerans have whip-like structures called **flagella**, which help them to move. Others are immotile.

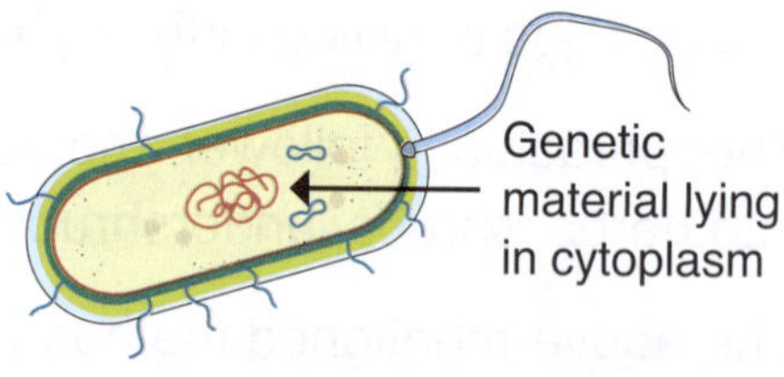


*Fig. 2.1 Bacteria lack a well-defined nucleus*

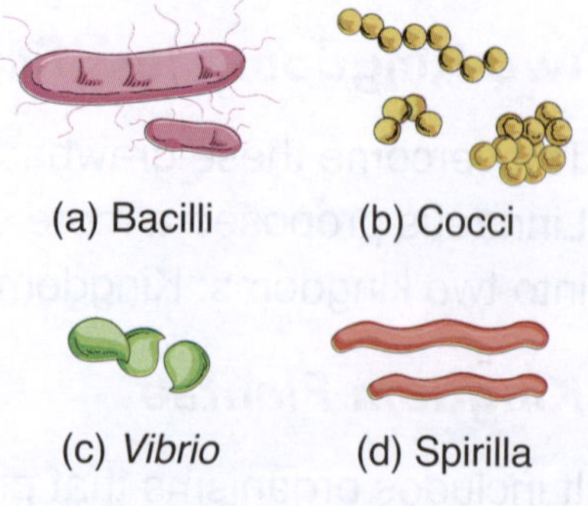


*Fig. 2.2 Different shapes of bacteria*

## Kingdom Protista

- They are unicellular.
- The genetic material of the cell is found inside a well-defined nucleus with a nuclear membrane.
- A few organisms are autotrophic, for example, diatoms and *Euglena*, while some are heterotrophic, for example, *Paramoecium* and *Amoeba*.
- They move with the help of special structures. Some of the special structures are cilia, flagella and pseudopodia.

  cilia – hair-like structures (for example, in *Paramoecium*, Fig. 2.3)

  flagella (singular: flagellum) – a whip-like structure (for example, in *Trypanosoma*, Fig. 2.4)

  **pseudopodia** – false limbs (for example, in *Amoeba*, Fig. 2.5)

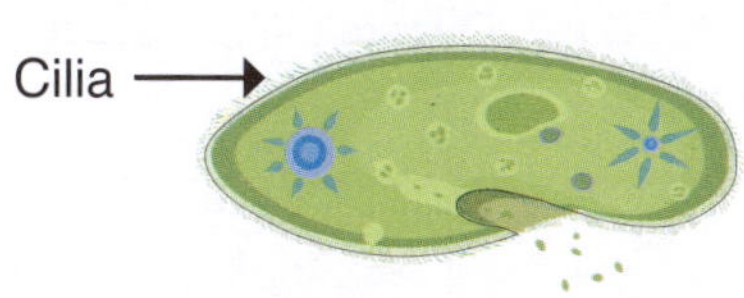


*Fig. 2.3 Paramoecium*

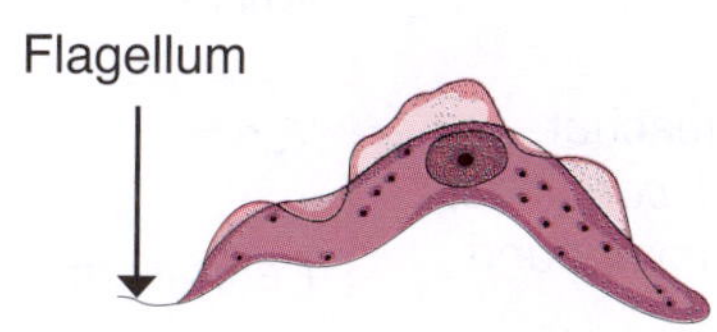


*Fig. 2.4 Trypanosoma*

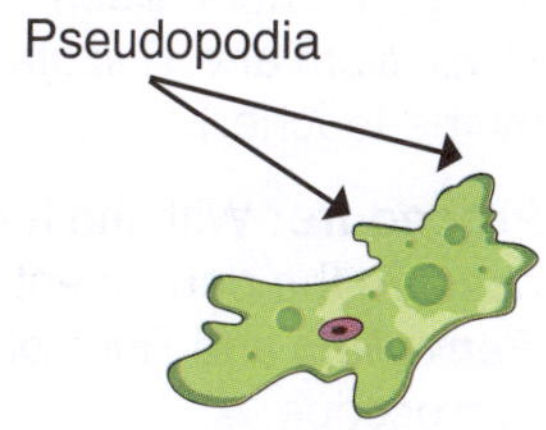


*Fig. 2.5 Amoeba*

## Kingdom Fungi

- Fungi are **non-green** organisms with cells having a well-defined nucleus. Some examples are moulds, mushrooms and yeast.
- Except yeast, all other fungi are multicellular.
- Their cells have a **cell wall** made of a substance called **chitin**.

**DO YOU KNOW?**

A new fungus was discovered in 2013 in Netherlands. It is called Orange Penicillium and named after the Dutch royal family, specifically the Prince of Orange.

- Fungi depend on other organisms for food (heterotrophs).
- The body of a multicellular fungus is known as **mycelium**, which is made up of thread-like structures known as **hyphae** (Fig. 2.6). Examples of fungi are *Mucor*, *Penicillium* (Fig. 2.7) and *Rhizopus* (Fig. 2.8).

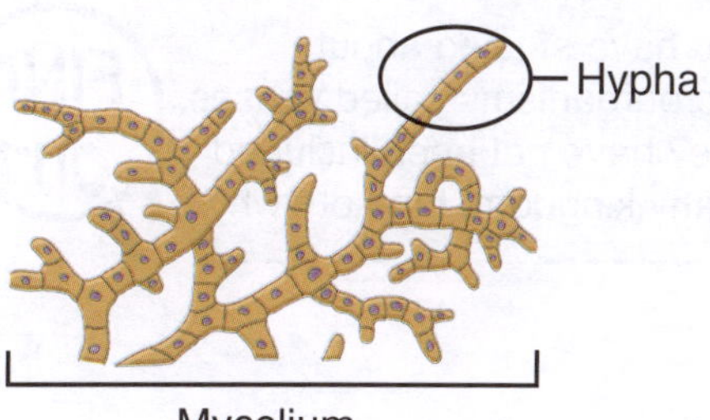


*Fig. 2.6 Structure of a fungus*

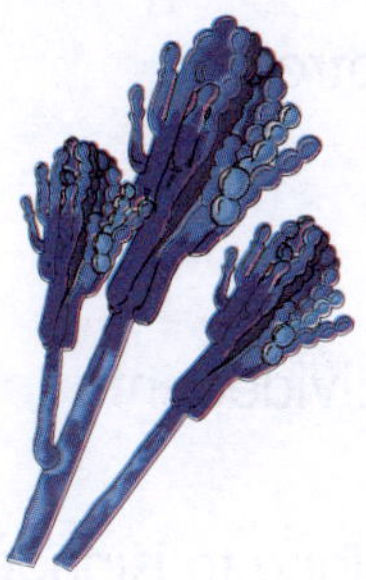

*Fig. 2.7 Penicillium*

*Fig. 2.8 Rhizopus*

## ACTIVITY 1

**Aim:** To observe a bread mould

**Materials required:** A piece of bread, a glass of water and compound microscope

**Procedure:**

1. Take a piece of bread and make it moist with a small amount of water.
2. Keep this moist bread in a warm place undisturbed for two to three days.

**Observation:** A greyish or blackish cotton-like mass will appear on the bread. This is called bread mould. Observe the mould under a microscope with the help of your teacher. Draw what you see in your notebook.

## ACTIVITY 2

**Aim:** To observe the structure of different fungi

**Materials required:** Compound microscope and permanent slides of *Mucor*, yeast, *Penicillium* and *Rhizopus* (to be provided by the teacher)

**Procedure:** With the help of your teacher, observe the permanent slides of *Mucor*, yeast, *Penicillium* and *Rhizopus* under a compound microscope.

**Observation:** Record your observations in the given table.

| Fungus | Multicellular/ Unicellular | Presence of hyphae (Yes or No) |
|---|---|---|
| *Mucor* | | |
| Yeast | | |
| *Penicillium* | | |
| *Rhizopus* | | |

## Kingdom Plantae

- They are **multicellular** and **autotrophic** organisms.
- All organisms within this kingdom have the pigment called **chlorophyll** and prepare their own food.
- They have a **cell wall** made of **cellulose**.
- The Kingdom Plantae is subdivided into various classes: thallophyta, bryophyta, pteridophyta, gymnosperms and angiosperms.

All plants belong to Kingdom Plantae.

**GREENATHON**

Gift a plant for every celebration. In this way, we can contribute to nature and celebrate life.

## Kingdom Animalia

- They are **multicellular** and heterotrophic organisms.
- They do not have a cell wall.
- The Kingdom Animalia is further divided into vertebrates and invertebrates.

All animals including human beings belong to Kingdom Animalia.

**FIND OUT**

You have studied about microorganisms called viruses. They have not been included in any kingdom. Find out why.

## QUICK REVISION

**Match the following.**

| | | | |
|---|---|---|---|
| 1. | Kingdom Plantae | a. | *Amoeba* |
| 2. | Kingdom Fungi | b. | Human being |
| 3. | Kingdom Protista | c. | Mint plant |
| 4. | Kingdom Animalia | d. | *Rhizopus* |
| 5. | Kingdom Monera | e. | Bacteria |

## GENERAL PLAN OF CLASSIFICATION

A scientifically classified group is known as a **rank** (plural: ranks) **or taxon** (plural: taxa). The hierarchy of groups is given below.

kingdom → phylum/division → class → order → family→ genus→ species

### Kingdom

This is the highest rank. As discussed earlier, Carolus Linnaeus had divided the living world into two kingdoms: plant and animal kingdom. However, modern science follows the five-kingdom classification system given by Whittaker.

### Phylum/Division

Each kingdom is further divided into many phyla (singular: phylum) based on similarities. For example, the plant kingdom is divided into two phyla, namely **cryptogams** (non-seed-bearing plants) and **phanerogams** (seed-bearing plants). Cryptogams include thallophyta, bryophyta and pteridophyta. Phanerogams include gymnosperms and angiosperms.

### Class

Organisms in a phylum are grouped into various classes. For example, animals that give birth to young ones and suckle them with milk are grouped under the class Mammalia. Angiosperms are divided into two classes called monocotyledons and dicotyledons. Monocotyledons such as rice, maize and wheat have one cotyledon. Dicotyledons such as rose, sunflower, mango, pea have two cotyledons.

### Order

Each class is divided into subgroups known as orders. For example, carnivorous animals are grouped under the order Carnivora. Plants that yield fibres are grouped under the order Malvales.

### Family

Under each order of animals and plants, there are many families. For example, cats are grouped under the family Felidae. Plants that bear rose-like flowers are grouped under the family Rosaceae.

## Genus

The animals and plants that belong to a family are divided into genera (singular: genus). For example, although tiger, lion and cat belong to the same family, they belong to different genera. Tigers and lions belong to the genus *Panthera* while cats belong to the genus *Felis*. The plant family Rosaceae has many genera. One of them is *Prunus*; it includes cherries and almonds.

### DO YOU KNOW?

An easy way to remember these taxonomic hierarchies is to remember this mnemonic:

**K**eep **P**ots **C**lean **O**r **F**amily **G**ets **S**ick

The bold letters denote the first letter of each taxonomic rank.

K: Kingdom; P: Phylum; C: Class; O: Order; F: Family; G: Genus; S: Species

## Species

The individual members of a genus that are capable of interbreeding or producing offsprings are known as **species** (plural: species). The species is the lowest ranked category in the hierarchy of classification and contains two parts in its scientific name. The first part is the name of the genus, written with the first letter in capital, and the second part is the name of the organism, written in small letters. This system of naming organisms is called the **binomial system of nomenclature.** The names of the genus and species are always printed in italics. For example, *Panthera tigris* (tiger) or *P. tigris*. When scientific names are handwritten, the genus and species names are underlined separately.

**Table 2.1 Taxonomical classification of some animals and plants**

| Taxonomical classification | |
|---|---|
| Kingdom: Animalia (Animals)<br>Phylum: Chordata (Vertebrate)<br>Class: Mammalia (Mammal)<br>Order: Carnivora (Carnivore)<br>Family: Felidae (Cat)<br>Genus: *Panthera*<br>Species: *Panthera tigris* (Tiger)  | Kingdom: Animalia (Animals)<br>Phylum: Chordata (Vertebrate)<br>Class: Mammalia (Mammal)<br>Order: Primates (Primate)<br>Family: Hominidae (Great ape)<br>Genus: *Homo*<br>Species: *Homo sapiens* (Human being)  |
| Kingdom: Plantae (Plants)<br>Phylum: Angiosperms<br>Class: Eudicots<br>Order: Malvales<br>Family: Malvaceae<br>Genus: *Hibiscus*<br>Species: *Hibiscus rosa-sinensis* (Hibiscus plant)  | Kingdom: Plantae (Plants)<br>Phylum: Gymnosperms<br>Class: Cycadopsida<br>Order: Cycadales<br>Family: Cycadaceae<br>Genus: *Cycas*<br>Species: *Cycas taitungensis* (Cycas plant)  |

## QUICK REVISION

**Fill in the blanks.**

1. A scientifically classified group is known as __________.
2. __________ is the highest rank in taxonomy.
3. Members of a genus capable of interbreeding or producing offsprings are called __________.
4. Cats are grouped under the family __________.
5. The scientific name of china rose plant is __________.

## USEFUL AND HARMFUL BACTERIA

Some examples of useful bacteria in different fields are given below.

- **Food processing:** *Lactobacillus* sp. is used for the fermentation of food products. It is also used to form organic acids in pickles.
- **Bioremediation:** *Alcanivorax borkumensis* are used to remove pollutants contaminating water and soil.
- **Pest control:** *Bacillus thuringiensis* (BT) is commonly used as an insecticide under different trade names.
- **Retting of fibres:** During the separation of fibres of jute, hemp and flax, *Clostridium butyricum* is used to ease the process of retting.
- **Biotechnology:** Bacteria is used in the production of many dietary supplements and pharmaceuticals. *E. coli* is used in the artificial synthesis of Vitamin $B_2$ and Vitamin K.
- **Digestion:** *E. coli* in humans and *Ruminococcus spp* in ruminants help in the digestion and absorption of food easily.
- **Nitrogen fixation:** *Rhizobium* bacteria found in the root nodules of leguminous plants (Fig. 2.9) helps in atmospheric nitrogen fixation.
- **Extremophiles:** Saprophytic bacteria feed on dead organic remains and aid in clean surrounding.
- **Medicine:** Antibiotics such as streptomycin are produced by the group of bacteria called *Streptococcus*.

*Fig. 2.9 Nodules of soybean roots*

Some examples of harmful bacteria are given below.

- **Disease causing:** A wide range of infections are caused by bacteria in humans, animals and plants. Impetigo, typhoid fever, cholera and tuberculosis are some of the examples of infections in humans. Anthrax and blackquarter are some bacterial diseases that occur in animals. Wildfire of tobacco, blight of beans and citrus stubborn disease are some bacterial infections that occur in plants.

- **Food spoilage:** Some of the decomposing bacteria present in soil attack and decompose the organic matter they encounter. This is the reason why tinned and packed food should not be consumed after the expiry date. Milk and milk products are equally exposed to different set of bacteria that spoil them.

## AMOEBA AND ITS PHYSIOLOGICAL PROCESS

*Amoeba* is one of the simplest organisms made up of just one simple cell. Some physiological processes in *Amoeba* are discussed below.

### Nutrition

*Amoeba* shows zootrophic mode of nutrition. It feeds by phagocytosis. It consumes algal cells and filaments, bacteria, desmids, flagellates, ciliates and small metazoans.

Nutrition involves a process of ingestion, digestion, absorption, assimilation, dissimilation and egestion. The process of ingestion is carried through the body surface with the help of **pseudopodia**.

On identification of food near itself, the pseudopodia extend and engulf the food, thus forming a food vacuole. Food is broken down inside the food vacuole and is absorbed. Undigested food is expelled through the cell membrane (Fig. 2.10).

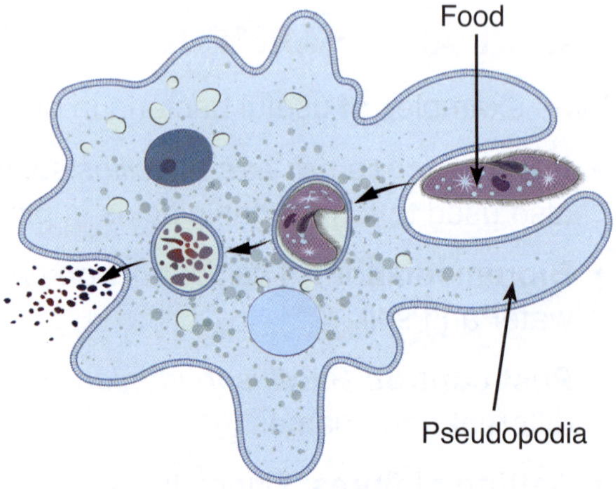


*Fig. 2.10 Feeding process in Amoeba*

### Locomotion

Pseudopodia is the locomotory organ in *Amoeba*. It is also called as **false foot**. This is the same organ that is also used to capture food. These are small to large or flat to thin projections formed by the cytoplasm along with the cell membrane on a temporary basis. The movement with these projections is known as amoebic movement.

### Respiration

*Amoeba* do not have any specialized respiratory system. It respires through the cell membrane. Exchange of oxygen and carbon dioxide occurs through diffusion through the cell membrane. Exchange of water molecules occurs through osmosis.

### Excretion

Ammonia and carbon dioxide are the two main waste materials produced by *Amoeba*. There is no special excretory organ system in *Amoeba*. Contractile vacuoles play an important role in the removal of waste from the body. Waste in the contractile vacuoles suspended in cytoplasm moves close to the plasma membrane where it burst opens, thereby releasing the waste out of the body.

## Reproduction

*Amoeba* reproduces by asexual mode of reproduction (binary fission). In binary fission (Fig. 2.11), a single cell divides into two identical cells (mitotic cell division). Some *Amoeba* also show multiple fission. In multiple fission, it forms a cyst, that protects the cell from harsh conditions. Once the conditions turn favourable, the cyst ruptures and continues to reproduce. Some cells also form spores while reproducing.

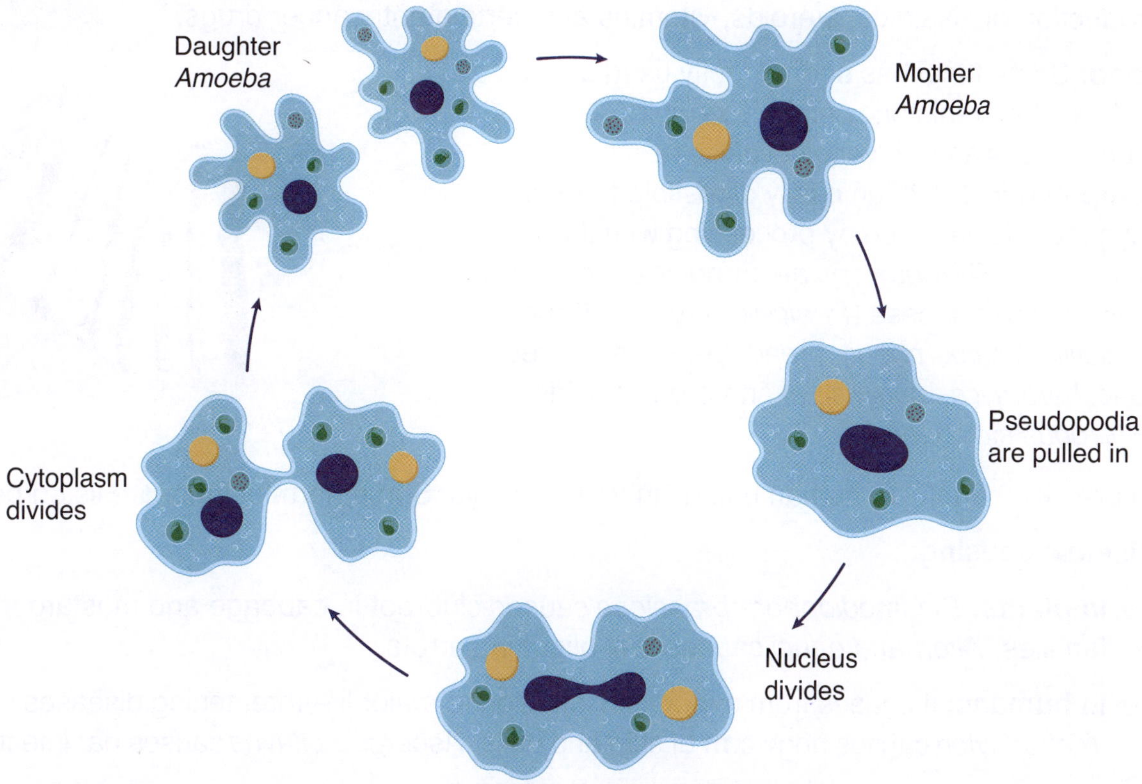


*Fig. 2.11 Binary Fission in Amoeba*

## FUNGI

Fungi may be unicellular or multicellular organisms devoid of chlorophyll.

### Nutrition

Fungi are heterotrophs. Fungi obtain nutrition in three different ways.

- **Saprophytic nutrition:** rely on dead and decaying matter for food
- **Parasitic nutrition:** rely on a living host for its food and harms the host
- **Mutualistic nutrition:** rely on a living host for food but do not harm the host

### Respiration

Fungi are mostly seen in dark places that are slightly moist and acidic in nature. Most of the fungi are obligate aerobes (requires oxygen to survive). Example: *Aspergillus* species. Few of them are obligate anaerobes (can live only in the absence of oxygen). Example: *Chytridiomycota* species. There are facultative anaerobes also (that can survive between the presence and absence of oxygen). Example: yeasts.

## Useful and Harmful Fungi

Like any other organisms, fungi has both useful and harmful effects. Some useful fungi are discussed below.

- **Medicine:** Fungi has been a boon in the discovery of antibiotics. *Penicillium notatum* is used in the production of Penicillin. This wonder drug was the first antibiotic that was discovered by Sir Alexander Fleming (1929). Other different fungi species are used in the production of alkaloids, steroids, vitamins and certain anti-cancer drugs.
- **Food:** Some fungi has been directly used as food as early as the prehistoric period. Example: *Agaricus brunnescens* and *Volveriella volvacea*.
  **Tempeh** (Fig. 2.12), an easily digestible form of soyabean, is prepared by processing with the fungi called *Rhizopus oryzae*. Fungi is used in the preparation of cheese (*Penicillium roquiforti* and *Penicillium camemberti*), bread (yeast), enzymes (*Saccharomyces cerevisiae*) and organic acids (*Rhizopus stolonifer*).

*Fig. 2.12 Tempeh*

Fungi are also harmful to human beings in various ways. Some harmful fungi are listed below.

- **Disease causing:**
  - **In plants:** *Plasmodiophora brassicae* causes clubroot in cabbage and mustard families. *Alternaria dauci* causes leaf blight in carrots.
  - **In humans:** It causes from minor skin infection to major life-threatening diseases. *Trichophyton* causes ringworm of skin and nails. *Aspergillus flavus* causes ear infections.
  - **In animals:** *Tinea rubrum* causes athlete foot. *Aspergillus* (a common mould) causes aspergillosis.
- **Spoilage of food:** *Mucor* (Fig. 2.13), *Aspergillus*, *Penicillium* and *Rhizopus* mostly affect and destroy different types of food.
- **Destruction of timber and goods:** Species of *Polyporus* and *Armillaria* (Fig. 2.14) cause wood rot in many trees. Different class of fungi also destroy paper, rubber, leather and jute.
- **Hallucinating drugs:** Certain extracts from the sclerotia of *Claviceps purpurea* cause hallucinating effect in humans when consumed. They damage the brain cells and cause distortion of perception in humans.

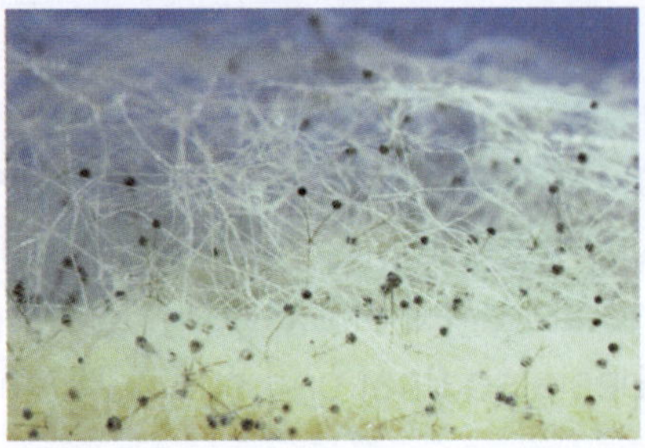

*Fig. 2.13 Mucor*

*Fig. 2.14 Armillaria*

## CONCEPT MAP

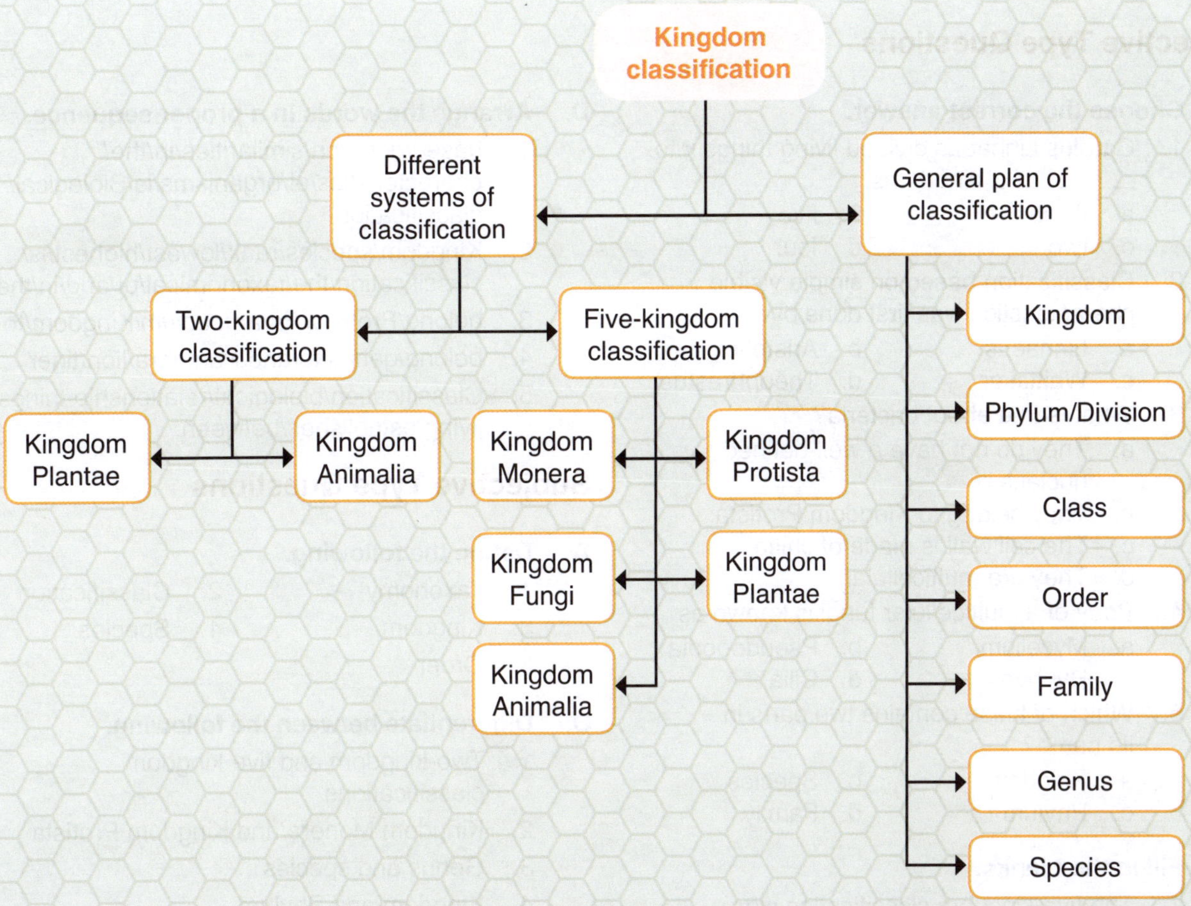


## KEYWORDS

**Classification:** grouping of living things based on common characteristics
**Taxonomy:** the branch of biology that systematically classifies living things
**Kingdom:** the largest group or division of classification
**Taxon:** each unit of classification also known as the rank
**Genus:** group of living things that have common characteristics
**Species:** individual members of the group genus that can interbreed to produce offspring

# Exercise

## Objective Type Questions

**A. Choose the correct answer.**

1. Carolus Linnaeus divided living things into ________ kingdoms.
   a three　　b. five
   c. two　　d. four
2. Classification based on simple visible characteristics was first done by
   a. Linnaeus　　b. Aristotle
   c. Whittaker　　d. Theophrastus
3. What is true about bacteria?
   a. They do not have a well-defined nucleus.
   b. They belong to Kingdom Protista.
   c. The cell wall is made of chitin.
   d. They are multicellular.
4. Body of a multicellular fungi is known as
   a. Mycelium　　b. Pseudopodia
   c. Hyphae　　d. Cilia
5. Which of these contains two parts in its name?
   a. Kingdom　　b. Species
   c. Phylum　　d. Family

**B. Fill in the blanks.**

1. The five-kingdom classification was proposed by ________ (RH Whittaker/ Carolus Linnaeus).
2. In Kingdom Plantae, the cell wall is made of ________ (chitin/cellulose).
3. Special structures for movement in *Paramoecium* are called ________ (flagella/cilia).
4. Organisms of Kingdom Fungi have cell walls made of ________ (cellulose/chitin).
5. Living things that belong to a particular kingdom are further divided into ________ (classes/phyla).

**C. Write T for True and F for False.**

1. Each class is further grouped into different orders.
2. Kingdom Protista has unicellular organisms that lack a well-defined nucleus.
3. *Homo sapiens* is the scientific name of cats.
4. Plants that bear rose-like flowers are grouped under the family Rosaceae.
5. Animals that give birth to young ones are grouped under Mammalia.

**D. Arrange the words in a proper sequence.**

1. based/done/on/similarities/in/the/ characteristics/of/organisms/is/Biological/ classification
2. Kingdom/species/rank/lowest/highest/is/ classification/the/taxonomical/of/and/in/the
3. belong/Protista/*Paramoecium*/Kingdom/to
4. belong/genus/to/and/Panthera/lion/tiger
5. Classification/biological/relationship/things/ living/establishes/between

## Subjective Type Questions

**A. Define the following.**

1. Taxonomy
2. Classification
3. Kingdom
4. Species
5. Order

**B. Differentiate between the following.**

1. Two-kingdom and five-kingdom classifications
2. Kingdom Monera and Kingdom Protista
3. Genus and species
4. Kingdom and Phylum
5. *Cycas* plant and *Hibiscus* plant

**C. Answer the following questions in brief.**

1. Write any two features of Kingdom Plantae.
2. Name any two kingdoms that consist of unicellular organisms.
3. Name the five kingdoms classified by RH Whittaker.
4. Name the ranks of classification.
5. The scientific name of an organism contains two parts. What do these parts represent?

**D. Answer the following questions in detail.**

1. What is classification? Give the advantages of classifying living things.
2. Write a note on classification based on simple visible characteristics. What are its drawbacks?
3. Write a note on the five-kingdom classification.
4. Write a note on the two-kingdom classification.
5. Explain the binomial system of nomenclature. Also, give some examples.

## Application-based Questions

What could be the advantage of using scientific names for organisms instead of common or popular names?

## Picture-based Questions

Observe the image given here and answer the following questions.

1. To which kingdom do these organisms belong?
2. Do all animal names start with the same species name?
3. Can mushroom be added to this kingdom?
4. Which of these species are similar to that of a mule?
5. Find out the names of the animal species given here.

# Skill Booster

**A.** **21CS:** Information Literacy | **BT:** Cognitive

Make a list of ten animals with their common names. Find out their scientific names. Collect their pictures and paste them in your scrapbook. Below every picture, write their common and scientific names.

**B.** **21CS:** Critical Thinking, Communication | **EL** | **BT:** Psychomotor

Observe slides of some unicellular microscopic organisms that use different types of structures such as pseudopodia, flagella and cilia for locomotion. Draw what you have observed. Discuss the same with your classmates.

**C.** **21CS:** Critical Thinking | **EL** | **BT:** Cognitive, Affective

Find out how scientific classification of organisms helps in the conservation of animals and plants. Map a plan on how you can contribute towards conservation of animals and plants.

**D.** **21CS:** Critical Thinking, Collaboration | **EL** | **CC:** English | **BT:** Cognitive, Affective

Go on a nature walk with your classmates and observe the diversity in plants and animals found in your area. Write a letter to the editor of your local newspaper discussing your observations and the steps that can be taken to conserve the biodiversity.

# Worksheet 2

Raju saw green patches on the stones at a riverbank. On touching the stones, he found them slimy. He assumed that it was grass that had grown on the rocks.

Discussing his experience with his friends, Raju told his friends that some grasses are slimy and are found only around waterbodies. One of the seniors among the group corrected him. His senior said: "It is not grass but *Algae*."

## My SEE Journal

A. How was the senior able to correct Raju's misconception? What would have happened if Raju was not corrected?

______________________________

______________________________

______________________________

______________________________

______________________________

B. How can one differentiate between *Algae* and grass?

______________________________

______________________________

## My SDG Journal

15 LIFE ON LAND

Like *Algae* and grass, there are many such organisms that are easily confused. Identify five such species and mark the distinguishing characteristics of such species.

______________________________

______________________________

______________________________

______________________________

______________________________

# 3 Classification of Animals

**Prior Knowledge**

- Kingdom classification
- Features of animals

**Learning Objectives**

- General characteristics of animals
- Characteristic features of invertebrates
- Characteristic features of vertebrates
- Classification of animals based on their food
- Classification of animals based on their habitat

## LET'S GET STARTED

Observe the images given below and write their respective Kingdom names.

1 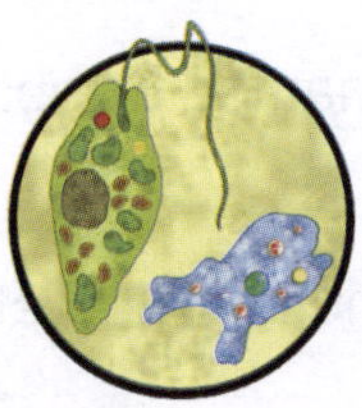

2 

3 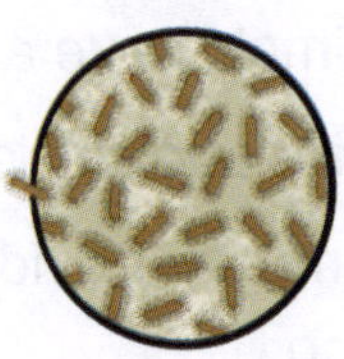

4 

5 

In the five-kingdom classification system, animals have been classified under Kingdom Animalia. The general characteristics of the organisms under Kingdom Animalia are given below.

- They are multicellular organisms. Their cells lack the cell wall and have a well-defined nucleus.
- They are heterotrophs, that is they cannot prepare their own food and depend on plants and other animals for food.
- They can move from one place to another in search of food and shelter.

The animal kingdom is further divided into many groups and subgroups. Let us learn more about the classification of animals in this chapter.

## CLASSIFICATION OF ANIMALS

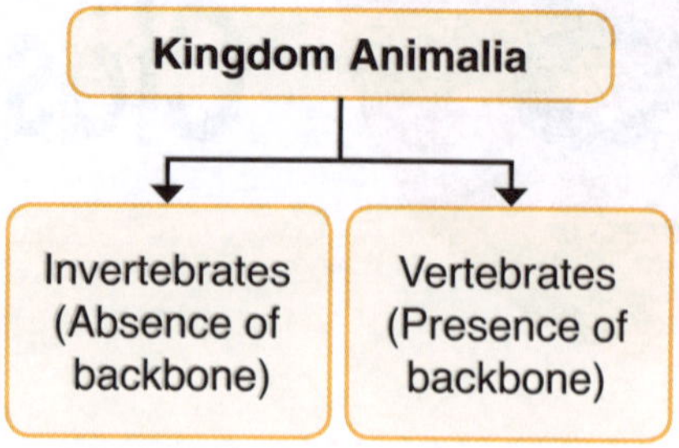


The animal kingdom is broadly divided into two groups based on the presence or absence of a backbone: vertebrates and invertebrates. A vertebral column or spinal cord gives a definite shape to the body. **Vertebrates** are animals with a backbone and **invertebrates** are animals without a backbone. There are more invertebrates identified than vertebrates.

## INVERTEBRATES

Invertebrates do not have a vertebral column. They are generally soft-bodied, delicate creatures. Most of them are aquatic. Invertebrates occur in a variety of body shapes such as round, flat, bag-shaped, thread-like, segmented, unsegmented and star-like. Invertebrates are divided into eight phyla (singular: phylum). Let us look at each phylum.

### Phylum Porifera (Sponges)

- In Greek, *porus* means 'pores' and *ferre* means 'to bear'.
- The bodies of these organisms are asymmetric.
- These animals have a lot of pores on their body; hence, they are named as sponges.
- Sponges live as a single entity as well as in colonies.
- They are mostly found in marine habitats. Some sponges are found in freshwater habitats too.
- They are usually found attached to the bottom of the sea and cannot move from one place to another place.
- They do not have a mouth; they take in water containing food and oxygen through tiny pores on their body.
- They have a large, central body cavity from where the water is released.
- Examples include Venus' flower basket, barrel sponge (Fig. 3.1) and tubular sponge (*Haliclona*, Fig. 3.2).

*Fig. 3.1 Barrel sponge*

*Fig. 3.2 Tubular sponge*

### Phylum Coelenterata (Cnidarians)

- In Greek, *knide* means 'nettle' or 'stinging cell'.
- The bodies of these organisms have radial symmetry (that is, their body can be divided into two equal halves through a central axis in more than one plane).

**TALK TIME**

Why should sponges be considered animals? How are sponges different from fungi?

- They are mostly found in marine habitats attached to the bottom of the ocean as well as floating on water.
- The mouth is the only opening in the body. The mouth is surrounded by finger-like projections known as **tentacles**. The tentacles have stinging cells called **cnidoblasts**; hence, they have been named cnidarians.
- The tentacles help them catch their prey and also to anchor themselves.
- Examples include *Hydra*, sea anemone (Fig. 3.3), jellyfish (Fig. 3.4) and corals.

*Fig. 3.3 Sea anemone*

*Fig. 3.4 Jellyfish*

**DO YOU KNOW?**

Jellyfish outdate dinosaurs and sharks in evolution, dating back to about 650 million years.

## Phylum Platyhelminthes (Flatworms)

- In Greek, *platys* means 'flat' and *helminth* means 'worms'.
- The body of flatworms is flat, thin and long.
- They are unsegmented (that is they have a smooth body surface) and bilaterally symmetrical (that is their body can be divided into two identical halves through only one plane).
- A few of them are found in freshwater, while most of them are animal parasites (live inside hosts).
- Their mouth is the only opening on the body through which they take in food and excrete wastes. They also have hook-like structures called **suckers** surround their mouth.
- Examples include *Planaria* (Fig. 3.5), tapeworm and blood fluke.

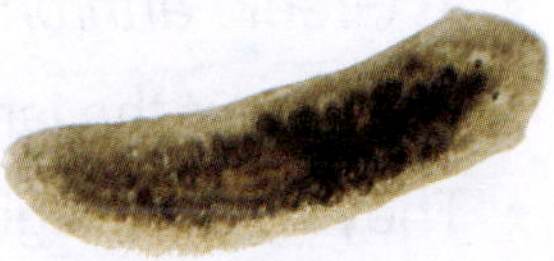

*Fig. 3.5 Planaria*

## Phylum Nemathelminthes or Nematoda (Roundworms)

- In Greek, *nema* means 'thread' and *helminth* means 'worm'.
- Roundworms are both free-living as well as parasitic.
- They are commonly found in animal intestines.
- The body of roundworms is long, unsegmented, cylindrical and bilaterally symmetrical.
- They have two openings in the body, a mouth and an anus.
- Examples include *Ascaris* (roundworm, Fig. 3.6), threadworm and hookworm.

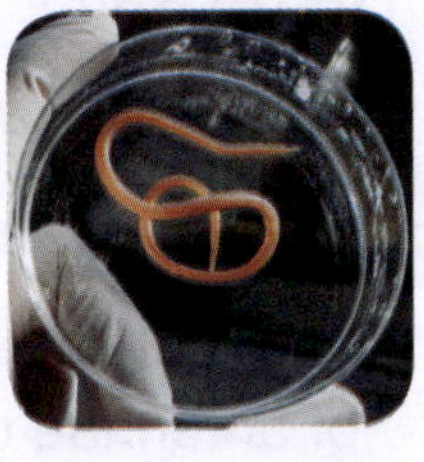

*Fig. 3.6 Ascaris*

## Phylum Annelida (Segmented Worms)

- In Greek, *annulus* means 'little ring' and *eidos* means 'form'.
- These organisms are found in moist soil and water.
- They have ring-like segments on the body surface.
- They have a body cavity and a digestive system with two openings: mouth and anus.
- They have special excretory organs known as **nephridia**.
- Examples include earthworm, leech, tubeworm and ragworm. Earthworms feed on dead and decaying substances in the soil. A leech (Fig. 3.7) is known as an **external parasite** as it sucks the blood of animals.

*Fig. 3.7 Leech*

## QUICK REVISION

**Write T for True and F for False.**

1. Organisms of Phylum Coelenterata have radial symmetry.
2. Hook-like structures called suckers are the characteristic features of Phylum Porifera.
3. Leech is an example of an internal parasite.
4. Hookworms belong to Phylum Platyhelminthes.
5. Nemathelminthes are commonly known as roundworms.

## Phylum Arthropoda (Animals That Have Jointed Legs)

- In Greek, *arthron* means 'a joint' and *podus* means 'foot'.
- It is one of the largest phyla. Arthropods are found in all habitats.
- They have a segmented body and jointed legs.
- The body is bilaterally symmetrical and has three main parts: head, thorax and abdomen.
- They have a protective hard shell covering their body called **exoskeleton**.
- They are further divided into four classes: crustaceans, insects, arachnids and myriapoda.

### Crustaceans

- In Greek, *crusta* means 'hard shell' and *acea* means 'belonging to'.
- They are mostly found in marine habitats.
- They have a fused head and thorax and two pairs of antennae on the head.
- They have an exoskeleton and many pairs of legs.
- Examples include lobster (Fig. 3.8), crab, shrimp and woodlouse (Fig. 3.9).

*Fig. 3.8 Lobster*

*Fig. 3.9 Woodlouse*

### *Insects*

- They are found in soil, water and air.
- Their body is differentiated into head, thorax and abdomen.
- All the body parts are covered by a single exoskeleton.
- They have three pairs of legs, a pair of antennae or feelers and usually two pairs of wings. There are some insects, that have one pair of wings, and some insects such as ant are wingless.
- Examples include grasshopper (Fig. 3.10), wasp, cockroach, bee (Fig. 3.11), mosquito and butterfly.

*Fig. 3.10 Grasshopper*

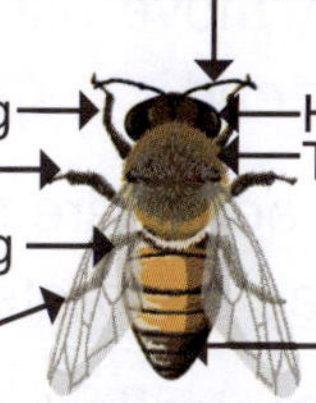


*Fig. 3.11 Bee*

### *Arachnids*

- In Greek, *arachne* means 'spider' (Fig. 3.12).
- They are found on land.
- Their head and thorax are fused.
- They do not have wings or antennae.
- They have a jaw-like structure called **pincer**, an exoskeleton and four pairs of legs.
- Examples include tick, mite, spider and scorpion (Fig. 3.13).

*Fig. 3.12 Spider*

*Fig. 3.13 Scorpion*

### *Myriapoda*

- In Greek, *myriad* means 'ten thousand' and *podus* means 'feet'.
- They are found on land.
- Their body is divided into several segments, with one or two pairs of legs per segment.
- Examples include centipede (one pair of legs per segment, Fig. 3.14) and millipede (two pairs of legs per segment, Fig. 3.15).

**DO YOU KNOW?**

A centipede's bite is poisonous.

*Fig. 3.14 Centipede*

*Fig. 3.15 Millipede*

## Phylum Mollusca (Animals That Have Shells and Soft Bodies)

- In Greek, *molluscus* means 'thin-shelled'.
- These soft-bodied animals are found in marine habitats, on seashores and on land.
- Their body is unsegmented and bilaterally symmetrical.
- Snails and oysters (Fig. 3.16) have a hard exoskeleton called **shell** to protect their soft bodies. Octopuses and slugs (Fig. 3.17) have a reduced internal shell.
- Examples include octopus, oyster, snail and squid.

*Fig. 3.16 Oyster*

*Fig. 3.17 Slug*

## Phylum Echinodermata (Animals With a Spiny Skin)

- In Greek, *derma* means 'skin'.
- They are found in marine habitats.
- Their body is covered with a hard skin containing spines, and they have an endoskeleton.
- They move with the help of tube feet with structures called **suckers** present at their end.
- The adults are radially symmetrical, while larvae are bilaterally symmetrical.
- Examples include sea urchin, starfish (Fig. 3.18), sea cucumber (Fig. 3.19) and brittle star.

*Fig. 3.18 Starfish*

*Fig. 3.19 Sea cucumber*

## QUICK REVISION

**Choose the correct answer.**

1. Identify the characteristic feature of arthropods.
   a. Endoskeleton  b. Jointed legs  c. Shells  d. Suckers
2. Which of the following has tube feet?
   a. Starfish  b. Octopus  c. Millipede  d. Centipede
3. Which of these molluscs has an internal shell?
   a. Sea urchin  b. Sea cucumber  c. Slugs  d. Brittle star
4. Insects belong to Phylum
   a. Annelida  b. Echinodermata  c. Arthropoda  d. Mollusca

## CLASSIFICATION OF VERTEBRATES

Vertebrates are animals with a backbone or a vertebral column that is made up of small bones called **vertebrae**. The vertebral column gives a definite shape and structure to organisms. In most animals, the vertebral column extends to form a tail. They have well-developed sense organs as well as nervous and digestive systems. They have muscles and skeleton and are capable of complex movements.

Vertebrates are further divided into five classes: pisces, amphibia, reptilia, aves and mammalia.

## Pisces (Animals That Live in Water)

- In Greek, *pisces* means 'fish'.
- They are found in aquatic habitats.
- They have special organs called gills to breathe, which help them take in the dissolved oxygen in water.

- They have a streamlined body and fins to help them swim.
- They are **cold-blooded**, that is their body temperature varies according to the temperature of the surroundings.
- Eggs of pisceans are laid in water.
- Examples are seahorse (Fig. 3.20), eel, rohu (Fig. 3.21) and shark.

*Fig. 3.20 Seahorse*

*Fig. 3.21 Rohu*

## Amphibia (Animals That Live Both on Land and in Water)

- In Greek, *amphi* means 'both' and *bios* means 'life'. They are found in both aquatic and terrestrial habitats.
- They breathe through their moist skin when present in water and through their lungs when present on land. Respiration through the skin is called **cutaneous respiration**.
- They are **cold-blooded** animals with smooth slippery skin.
- They reproduce by laying eggs in water.
- Examples are frog, salamander (Fig. 3.22) and newt (Fig. 3.23)

*Fig. 3.22 Salamander*

*Fig. 3.23 Newt*

## Reptilia (Animals That Crawl)

- In Greek, *reptilis* means 'to creep'.
- Reptiles are found both on land and in water, but they are better suited to land than amphibians.
- They are **cold-blooded** animals. They breathe through their lungs.
- Their skin is covered with **scales** or **scutes** (such as the shell of a tortoise and the bony shield of a crocodile).
- They lay eggs on land and their young ones directly hatch into young adults without going through the larval stage.
- Examples are turtle (Fig. 3.24), lizard and crocodile (Fig. 3.25).

*Fig. 3.24 Turtle*

*Fig. 3.25 Crocodile*

## Aves (Animals With Feathers)

- In Greek, *aves* means 'birds'.
- They share a varied habitat such as land, water and trees.
- They breathe through lungs.
- They are **warm-blooded** animals, that is their body temperature does not change with the change in the temperature of their surroundings.

**DO YOU KNOW?**

Salamanders can regenerate a lost limb or tail.

- Most of them have forelimbs modified into a pair of wings to fly.
- They have a streamlined body covered with feathers and hollow bones that help them fly.
- They have two legs (hindlimbs) to walk, perch and catch their prey.
- They reproduce by laying eggs.
- They have no teeth, but have a beak instead.
- Examples include parrot, ostrich (Fig. 3.26) and crow (Fig. 3.27).

Fig. 3.26 Ostrich

Fig. 3.27 Crow

Some birds cannot fly. These are known as **flightless birds**. The smallest flightless bird is the island rail and the largest is the ostrich. Penguin, emu, cassowary, kiwi and rhea are other examples of flightless birds.

## Mammalia (Animals That Suckle Their Young Ones)

- In Greek, *mammalis* means 'of the breast'.
- Mammals are highly evolved animals among vertebrates.
- In mammals, females have mammary glands that produce milk. They suckle their babies after giving birth.
- They are found on land and in water.
- They are **warm-blooded** animals with hair on their skin. They breathe through lungs.
- They have a well-developed brain. They also have external ears, nose, eyes and a set of teeth.
- They usually have two pairs of limbs. Some use all the four limbs as legs, while others use one pair as legs and the other pair as hands.
- Examples include human being, monkey, cat, dog, cow (Fig. 3.28) and horse (Fig. 3.29).

Fig. 3.28 Cow and calf

Fig. 3.29 Horse and pony

**DO YOU KNOW?**

The duck-billed platypus is a mammal that lays eggs. It lives in a semi-aquatic habitat.

Bats are the only mammals that can fly. They have webbed wings that are an extension of their digits or fingers.

## QUICK REVISION

**Choose the correct answer.**

1. Which group of animals lives both on land and in water?
   a. Aves b. Amphibia c. Reptilia d. Mammalia
2. The animals belonging to this phylum have hairs on their body.
   a. Reptilia b. Mammalia c. Aves d. Amphibia
3. Cutaneous respiration is breathing through
   a. gills b. lungs c. skin d. mouth
4. The crocodile belong to the class
   a. Mammalia b. Aves c. Reptilia d. Amphibia

## CLASSIFICATION BASED ON THE TYPE OF NUTRITION

Nutrition is consuming (taking in) essential nutrients such as carbohydrates, proteins, fats, vitamins and minerals. All animals need these nutrients for survival. The mode of consuming these nutrients varies across organisms. Animals are broadly divided into two groups based on the type of nutrition: holozoic and parasitic.

**Holozoic animals** consume plants or other animals as food. These animals are divided into three subgroups: herbivorous, carnivorous and omnivorous animals.

- **Herbivorous animals** eat only plant and plant products. Examples include cow, sheep, goat, giraffe, elephant, deer and bison.
- **Carnivorous animals** eat flesh of other animals. Examples include lion, tiger, cheetah, leopard, wolf and frog.
- **Omnivorous animals** eat both animals and plants. Examples include chimpanzee, bear, crow and human being.

**Parasitic animals** such as roundworms, tapeworms and head louse live inside the body or on the body surface of host animals and derive nutrition from them.

## CLASSIFICATION BASED ON HABITAT

Living things are adapted to their natural habitat. Animals can be classified into three groups based on the type of habitat: terrestrial, aquatic and arboreal.

**Terrestrial Animals:** Animals that live entirely or predominantly on land are known as terrestrial animals. Ant, snail, tiger, elephant, cow and dog are the examples of terrestrial animals.

**Aquatic Animals:** Animals that live entirely or predominantly in water are known as aquatic animals. Fish, octopus, dolphin, whale and squid are the examples of aquatic animals.

**Arboreal Animals:** Animals that live on trees most of the time are known as arboreal animals. Monkey, squirrel, koala bear, panda and lemur are arboreal animals.

## CONCEPT MAP

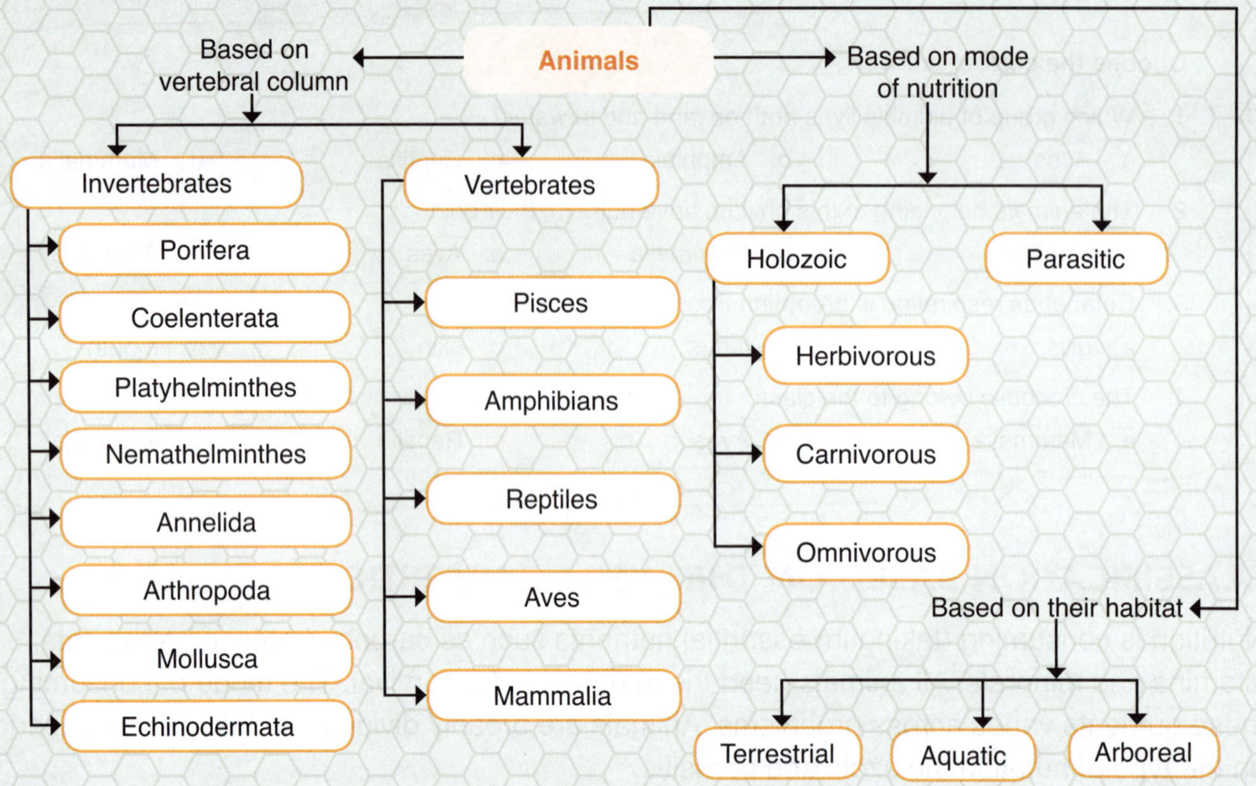


## KEYWORDS

**Invertebrates:** animals that do not have a vertebral column or spinal cord

**Vertebrates:** animals that have a vertebral column or spinal cord

**Tentacles:** the finger-like projections that surround the mouths of coelenterates

**Nephridia:** the excretory organs in organisms of Phylum Annelida

**Exoskeleton:** a hard outer covering on the body of certain organisms

**Pincer:** a jaw-like structure in Arachnids

**Shell:** a hard exoskeleton found in animals belonging to Phylum Mollusca

**Suckers:** the tube-like feet found in animals belonging to Phylum Echinodermata

**Amphibians:** animals that can live both on land and in water

**Mammals:** animals that suckle their young ones

**Terrestrial animals:** animals that live entirely or predominantly on land

**Aquatic animals:** animals that live entirely or predominantly in water

**Arboreal animals:** animals that live on trees most of the time

# Exercise

## Objective Type Questions

**A. Choose the correct answer.**

1. Which of these belongs to Phylum Porifera?
   a. *Haliclona* b. Jellyfish
   c. Roundworm d. *Hydra*
2. Finger-like projections around the mouth of cnidarians are called
   a. flagella b. tentacles
   c. cilia d. none of these
3. Which of the following is a characteristic feature of reptiles?
   a. Webbed feet b. Scaled skin
   c. Feather d. Tentacles
4. Excretory organs called nephridia are present in
   a. Arthropoda b. Annelida
   c. Cnidarians d. Porifera
5. Animals that have hollow bones and streamlined bodies covered with feathers belong to
   a. Mammalia b. Reptilia
   c. Aves d. Amphibia

**B. Fill in the blanks.**

1. Cutaneous respiration in frogs takes place through the ______________ (skin/gills).
2. Animals that live on trees most of the time are known as ______________(aquatic/arboreal) animals.
3. ______________ (Mammals/Amphibians) reproduce by laying eggs.
4. Soft-bodied animals with hard shells are grouped under Phylum ______________ (Mollusca/Annelida).
5. ______________ (Annelids/Arachnids) have a jaw-like structure called pincer.

**C. Write T for True and F for False.**

1. Frogs are cold-blooded animals.
2. Crocodiles lay eggs in water.
3. Tentacles are present in flatworms.
4. Turtles are reptiles.
5. Animals of Phylum Porifera have radially symmetrical bodies.

**D. Arrange the words in a proper sequence.**

1. backbone/with/are/called/vertebrates/Animals
2. Porifera/all/their/pores/Phylum/have/over/body
3. Phylum/cnidoblasts/have/Coelenerata
4. nephridia/called/excretory/Annelida/Phylum/special/organs/have
5. eggs/cold-blooded/reptiles/animals/lay/like

## Subjective Type Questions

**A. Define the following.**

1. Vertebrates
2. Invertebrates
3. Exoskeleton
4. Holozoic nutrition
5. Cutaneous respiration

**B. Differentiate between the following.**

1. Porifera and Cnidarian
2. Platyhelminthes and Nemathelminthes
3. Amphibians and Pisces
4. Arachnids and insects
5. Molluscs and Echinoderms

**C. Answer the following questions in brief.**

1. Name the three body parts of an insect.
2. What do you mean by an exoskeleton?
3. Explain the features of Echinodermata in brief.
4. What are pincers?
5. What are tentacles?

**D. Answer the following questions in detail.**

1. Write a note on Phylum Annelida.
2. Write the characteristics of Phylum Coelenterata.
3. List the eight phyla of invertebrates. Give one example of each.
4. Explain the characteristic features of Aves.
5. Write short notes on amphibians and reptiles.

## Application-based Question

What are the different ways by which mammals maintain their body temperature?

## Picture-based Questions

Observe the images given below and answer the following questions.

1. To which phylum does the Shrew belong?
2. To which phylum does the blue whale belong?
3. List any two features of shrews.
4. List any two features of blue whales.
5. What is the one contradictory feature of these two species?

# Skill Booster

**A.** 21CS: Communication | EL | AI | BT: Affective, Psychomotor

Observe the specimens of animals that are preserved in the laboratory. Draw any four of them in your practical notebook. Discuss the same with your classmates.

**B.** 21CS: Information Literacy | CC: Computer Science | BT: Cognitive

Marsupials are mammals that are born incomplete. The young ones are carried by their mothers and nurtured until completely developed. Find out more about marsupials. Prepare a presentation based on your findings.

# Worksheet 3

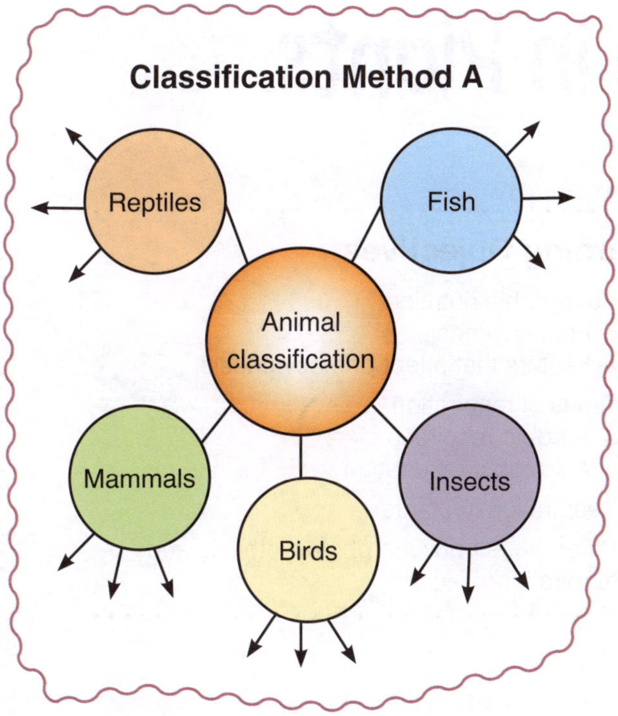

## My SEE Journal

A. Which method of classification would be better for understanding? Justify.

______________________________

______________________________

B. Do you think teaching with the help of aids helps you understand better? Substantiate.

______________________________

______________________________

C. Write the classification hierarchy and scientific name for red fox.

______________________________

______________________________

## My SDG Journal

15 LIFE ON LAND

A. How is this classification helpful to us?

______________________________

______________________________

B. What would happen if the animals are not classified?

______________________________

______________________________

C. Which is the latest inclusion in the classification chart of animals?

______________________________

______________________________

# 4 Photosynthesis and Respiration in Plants

**Prior Knowledge**

- Plant kingdom
- Uses of plants
- Life processes

**Learning Objectives**

- Autotrophic nutrition
  - Photosynthesis
  - Factors that affect photosynthesis
- Types of respiration
  - Aerobic respiration
  - Anaerobic respiration
- Respiration in plants
- Differences between photosynthesis and respiration

## LET'S GET STARTED

Observe the images given below. Tick the organisms that can perform photosynthesis. Can you name these organisms?

1 

2 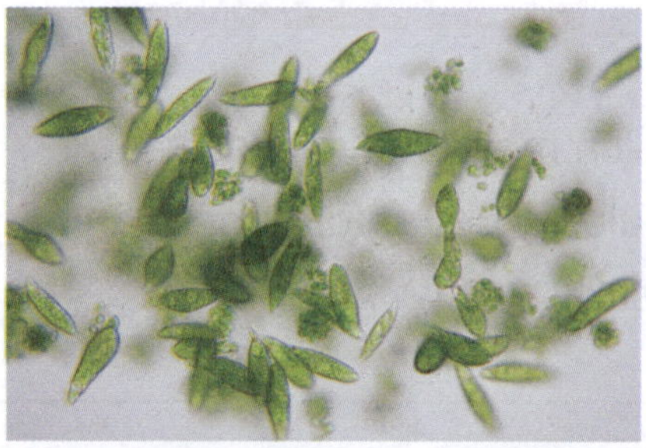

3 

4 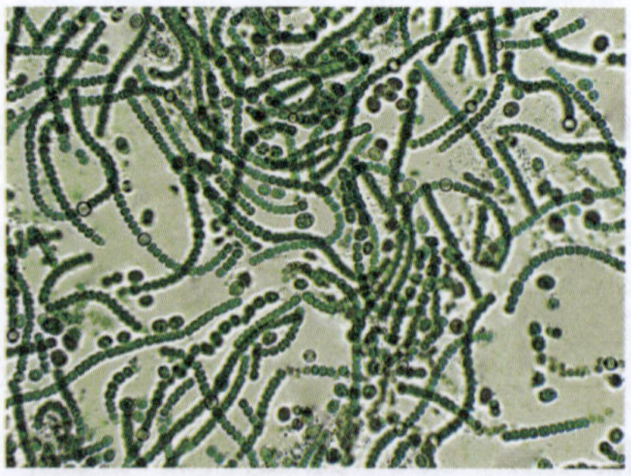

To keep themselves alive, all living organisms perform basic functions known as life processes. These life processes include respiration, nutrition, excretion, response to stimuli, growth and repair, and reproduction.

In this chapter, we will learn about the processes of photosynthesis and respiration in plants.

## AUTOTROPHIC NUTRITION

Organisms capable of preparing their own food are known as autotrophs. This type of nutrition is called **autotrophic nutrition**.

We know that green plants prepare their own food through the process of **photosynthesis**. Therefore, they are also called **producers** or **autotrophs**. Photosynthesis takes place in all the green parts of a plant. The cells in the green parts of a plant contain an organelle called **chloroplast**, which contains a green pigment called **chlorophyll**. This pigment helps in trapping sunlight, the main source of energy. Water is drawn from the roots to the leaf blades. The underside of leaves has tiny pores called **stomata** through which carbon dioxide is drawn from the air.

Some plants lack chlorophyll or grow in areas where they do not get enough sunlight. Such plants depend on other organisms for their food. This type of nutrition in which nutrients are obtained from other organisms is called **heterotrophic nutrition**. Organisms that follow the heterotrophic mode of nutrition are called **heterotrophs**.

## PHOTOSYNTHESIS

Green plants use sunlight, chlorophyll, water and carbon dioxide to photosynthesize (Fig. 4.1) ('photo' means 'light' and 'synthesize' means 'to make').

$$\text{Carbon dioxide + Water} \xrightarrow[\text{Chlorophyll}]{\text{Sunlight}} \text{Glucose + Oxygen + Water}$$

$$6CO_2 + 12H_2O \xrightarrow[\text{Chlorophyll}]{\text{Sunlight}} C_6H_{12}O_6 + 6O_2 + 6H_2O$$

Six molecules of carbon dioxide and six molecules of water react in the presence of chlorophyll and sunlight to give one molecule of glucose and six molecules of oxygen. Oxygen and glucose thus formed are the products of photosynthesis. Oxygen is released through the stomata, and glucose is stored as starch and used by the plant for various metabolic activities.

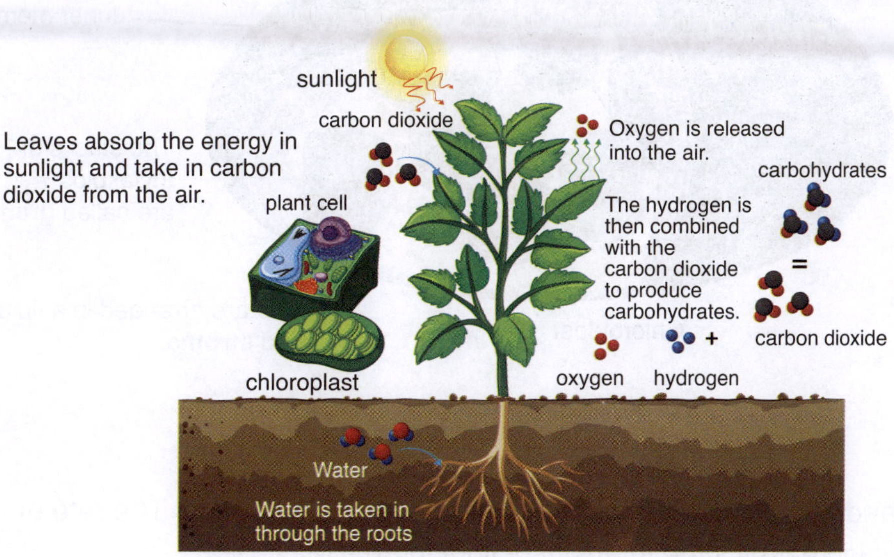


*Fig. 4.1 Green plants prepare their own food*

## Factors That Affect Photosynthesis

The factors that affect photosynthesis are light, carbon dioxide, temperature, water and minerals.

**Light:** The chlorophyll or the green pigment present in the leaves of plants helps in the absorption of sunlight.

Leaf cells have special chlorophyll-containing structures called **chloroplasts**. The structure of chloroplasts is explained in Figure 4.2.

Chlorophyll absorbs sunlight and converts it into chemical energy, which is then used by plants to prepare food in the leaves.

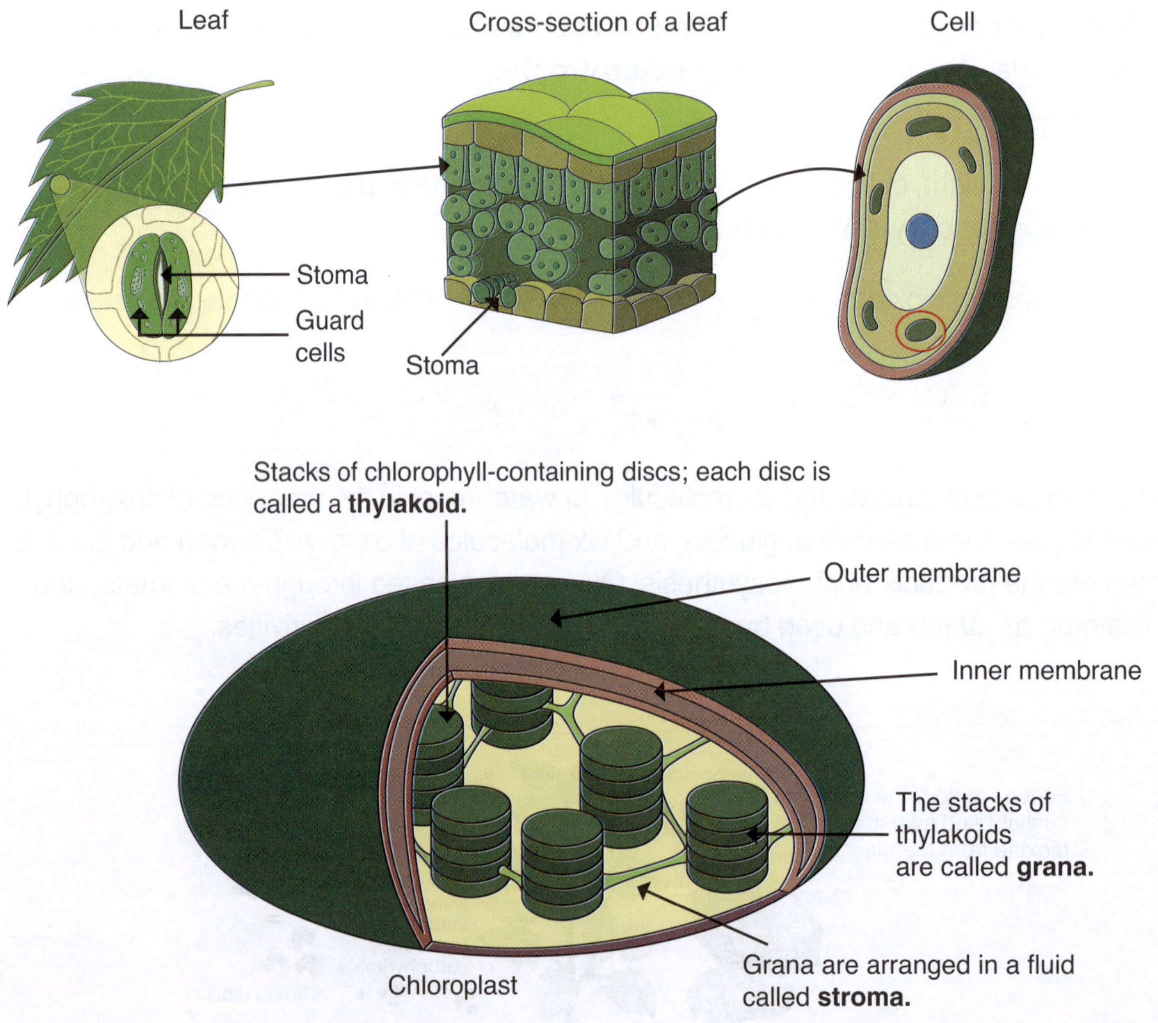


*Fig. 4.2 Chloroplasts in a plant cell*

The intensity and duration of light affect the rate of photosynthesis. The rate of photosynthesis increases if the intensity of light increases.

## ACTIVITY 1

**Aim:** To test for the presence of starch in a leaf after photosynthesis

**Note:** *This activity is to be performed as a teacher demonstration.*

**Materials required:** Iodine, dropper, Bunsen burner, test tube, beaker, alcohol, white tray and a potted plant

**Procedure:**

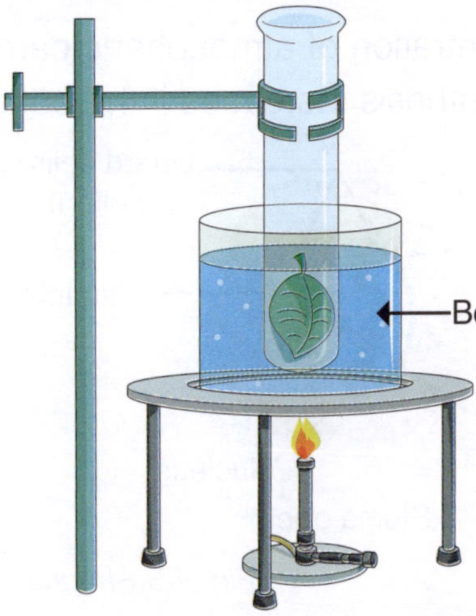


1. Keep a healthy potted plant in dark for about 24–48 hours.
2. Pluck a leaf out of this plant before you keep it out in sunlight. This is leaf A (the control).
3. Now, pluck another leaf from the plant after it has been in sunlight for at least one to two hours. This is leaf B (the experimental leaf).
4. Pour alcohol in a test tube and immerse the two leaves in it. Keep the test tube inside a 1-litre beaker containing water and heat it.

   (*Caution: Alcohol is highly inflammable. It should never be heated directly.*)
5. When the alcohol starts to boil, green colour comes off the leaves and the chlorophyll starts to dissolve in the alcohol.
6. Take out the leaves and wash them in water to remove the alcohol.
7. Place the leaves on the white tray and add a drop of iodine to the leaves using the dropper.

**Observation:** Leaf A takes the colour of iodine as it was decolourized earlier and then iodine was added to it. So, it will appear brown. Whereas in Leaf B, the colour changes to blue–black, thereby indicating the presence of starch in it.

## ACTIVITY 2

**Aim:** To prove that light is required for the process of photosynthesis

**Materials required:** A potted plant, black paper and materials for the starch test

**Procedure:**

1. Keep a potted plant in a dark room for 24–48 hours.
2. Before keeping it out in sunlight, cover one of the leaves with black paper.
3. Leave the experimental set-up in the sunlight for 6–8 hours.
4. Pluck two leaves, the one that was covered with black paper and any other healthy leaf from the plant.
5. Now, test the leaves for starch as described in Activity 1.

**Observation:** The leaf covered with black paper shows a negative result for the starch test, whereas the other healthy leaf tests positive for starch.

**Conclusion:** This experiment shows that sunlight is required for the process of photosynthesis.

**Carbon dioxide:** The leaves of plants absorb carbon dioxide from the atmosphere. Carbon dioxide is absorbed through minute openings on the underside of leaves known as **stomata**.

Stomata (singular: stoma) are surrounded by bean-shaped guard cells on either side (Fig. 4.3). The water that is taken up into the leaves enters the guard cells and makes them swell. The guard cells expand and are pulled apart, thus creating a gap or an opening, which we refer to as a stoma. When water is lost from the guard cells, they shrink and the gap is closed. Gases such as carbon dioxide and oxygen are exchanged via stomata.

The concentration of atmospheric carbon dioxide affects the rate of photosynthesis. The rate of photosynthesis increases if the concentration of carbon dioxide is high.

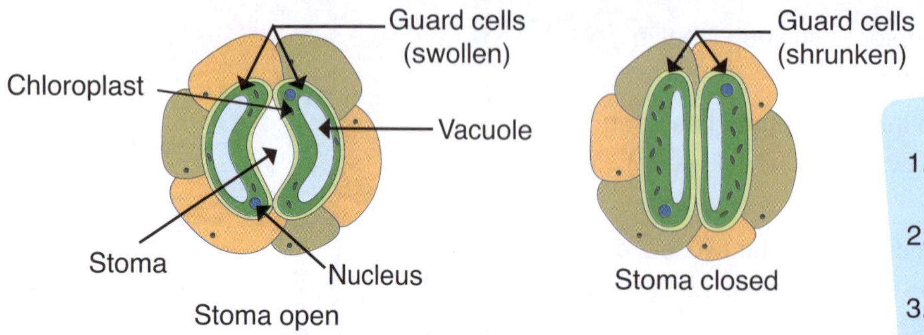


*Fig. 4.3 Structure of stomata*

## TALK TIME

1. What do you conclude from Activity 2?
2. Why did Leaf A not change its colour whereas Leaf B did?
3. Why was the potted plant kept in dark for 24–48 hours?

**Temperature:** The temperature between 20°C and 30°C is optimum for photosynthesis. If the temperature is higher than the optimum temperature range, the enzymes involved in the process are destroyed.

**Water and minerals:** The root system in plants helps in the absorption of water and minerals from the soil. These are carried to the other parts of the plant through tubular structures called **xylem**.

Stomata open when water is available. Availability of water increases the rate of photosynthesis, whereas reduced water availability reduces the rate of photosynthesis as well as closes the stomata, thus stopping the exchange of gases.

## ACTIVITY 3

**Aim:** To prove that chlorophyll is required for photosynthesis

**Materials required:** Iodine solution, a potted plant with variegated leaves and materials for starch test

*A plant with variegated leaves*

**Procedure:**

1. Keep the potted plant in dark for 24 to 48 hours. Then expose it to sunlight for 4–6 hours.
2. Take a large, healthy leaf from the plant.
3. Draw the leaf in your notebook, carefully marking the areas on the leaf where chlorophyll is not present (or vice versa).
4. Perform the starch test as given in Activity 1.
5. Compare the colour of iodine seen on the leaf with your diagram. Where do you see the blue–black portions on the leaf?

**Observation:** Only those parts of a leaf that are green in colour due to the presence of chlorophyll show the colour change in the starch test.

**Conclusion:** Chlorophyll is required for plants to make their food.

## ACTIVITY 4

**Aim:** To demonstrate that carbon dioxide is required for photosynthesis

**Materials required:** Potted plant, two conical flasks, split corks, stands, water, potassium hydroxide and materials for starch test

**Procedure:**

Keep the potted plant in dark/indoors for 24–48 hours.

Use this plant as given below.

1. Take two conical flasks. One conical flask marked A should contain potassium hydroxide and another marked B should contain water.
2. Insert one leaf of the potted plant into each flask through the split corks, as shown in the picture. Arrange the set-up as shown in the figure. Take care not to immerse the leaves in the liquids.
3. Leave the experimental set-up near a window or in sunlight for a few hours.
4. Pluck out both the leaves from the plant and test for starch as discussed in Activity 1.

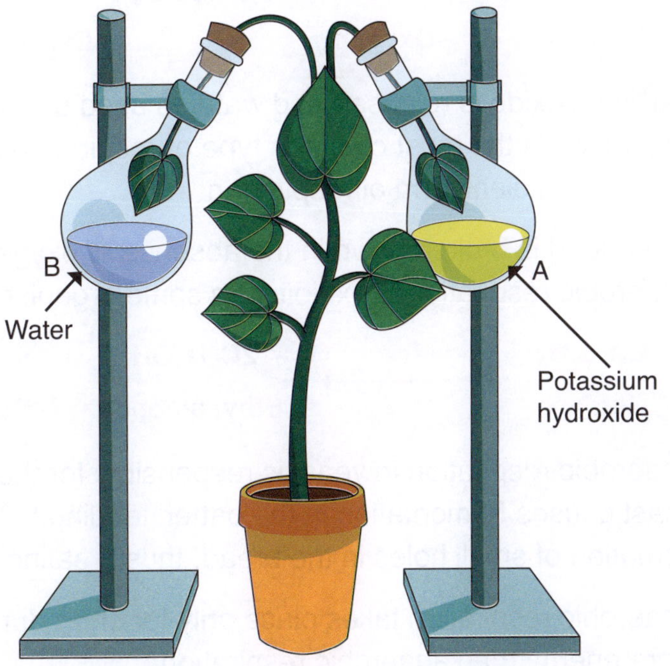


**Observation:** The leaf from the set-up marked B turns blue–black due to the presence of starch, whereas the other one from flask A does not show any change in its colour.

**Conclusion:** Carbon dioxide necessary for photosynthesis is absorbed by potassium hydroxide in flask A. Photosynthesis does not take place due to the absence of carbon dioxide. Starch is not formed. This is confirmed by the negative result of the starch test. Flask B contains water and thus, $CO_2$ is available. Starch is formed, and it is confirmed by the positive result of the starch test.

## RESPIRATION

All living beings need food as a source of energy to carry out various life processes. The process of digestion breaks down food into simple molecules such as glucose. This glucose produced during digestion needs to be further broken down to produce energy. This is done through the process of respiration. The process of **respiration** involves the oxidation of food (glucose) to produce water, carbon dioxide and energy.

**Glucose + Oxygen ⟶ Water + Carbon dioxide + Energy**

The energy released is stored and used by the body in the form of a chemical substance called **adenosine triphosphate** (ATP). ATP is also called the **energy currency** of a cell.

## TYPES OF RESPIRATION

Intake of oxygen is one of the first steps of respiration. However, respiration can happen in the absence of oxygen also.

When food (glucose) is broken down in the presence of oxygen, it is called **aerobic respiration**.

| $C_6H_{12}O_6$ | + | $6O_2$ | $\longrightarrow$ | $6CO_2$ | + | $6H_2O$ | + | 38 ATP |
|---|---|---|---|---|---|---|---|---|
| Glucose | | Oxygen | | Carbon dioxide | | Water | | Energy |

Carbon dioxide is released and water is used up for other cellular functions. Aerobic respiration is the most common type of respiration exhibited by most organisms. It is also the most efficient form of respiration.

When food is broken down in the absence of oxygen, it is called **anaerobic respiration**. Anaerobic respiration is exhibited in some organisms such as yeast and certain bacteria.

| $C_6H_{12}O_6$ | $\longrightarrow$ | $2C_2H_5OH$ | + | $2CO_2$ | + | 2 ATP |
|---|---|---|---|---|---|---|
| Glucose | | Ethyl alcohol | | Carbon dioxide | | Energy |

Anaerobic respiration in yeast is responsible for the fluffiness of bread, idli and dosa batter. Yeast causes fermentation in the batter, leading to the escape of carbon dioxide and formation of small holes in the bread, thus creating fluffiness.

Anaerobic respiration takes place only for short durations. Aerobic respiration produces more energy than anaerobic respiration.

The muscle cells in our body normally carry out aerobic respiration. When we run fast or exercise vigorously, the muscle cells work faster and require instant energy. To meet this energy demand, the muscle cells switch to anaerobic respiration. In this case, instead of alcohol, lactic acid is produced. The partial breakdown of glucose produces lactic acid.

$$\text{Glucose} \longrightarrow \text{Lactic acid} + \text{Energy}$$

**Table 4.1 Differences between aerobic and anaerobic respiration**

| Aerobic Respiration | Anaerobic Respiration |
|---|---|
| Oxidation of glucose takes place in the presence oxygen | Oxidation of glucose takes place in the absence of oxygen |
| Occurs in plants, animals, human beings and microorganisms | Occurs in organisms under the condition of insufficient oxygen and in some microorganisms |
| Glucose is broken down completely | Glucose is broken down partially |
| More energy is released | Less energy is released |

## ACTIVITY 5

**Aim:** To prove that anaerobic respiration takes place in the absence of oxygen, while aerobic respiration takes place in the presence of oxygen

**Materials required:** Germinating seeds, limewater, two test tubes, two conical flasks, stoppers, bent glass tubes, short tubes, oil, warm water, yeast and glucose

**Procedure:** Distribute limewater equally into the test tubes (take the help of your teacher to make sure that it does not come in contact with the carbon dioxide in the air).

**Experimental set-up 1:**

1. Place 30 g of germinating seeds in one of the conical flasks.
2. Cover the conical flask with the two-holed stopper.
3. Insert a bent glass tube into one hole and the short tube into the other hole.
4. Connect the bent tube to a test tube having limewater through the one-holed stopper.

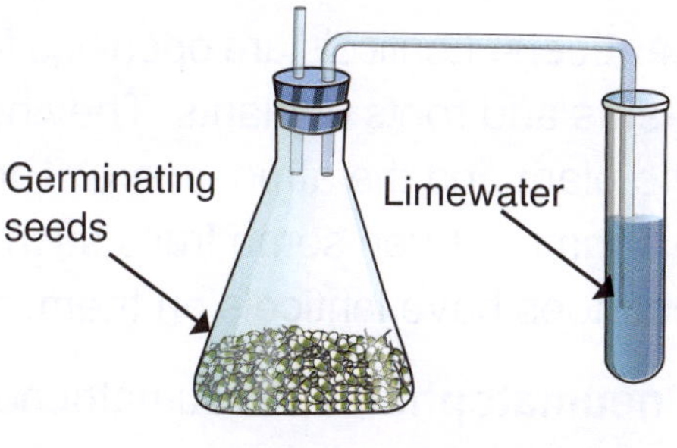


*Experimental set-up 1*

**Experimental set-up 2:**

1. Pour warm water into another conical flask and add glucose and yeast.
2. Mix well. Pour oil over the surface of the solution (to prevent the entry of air).
3. Do not shake the set-up once the oil is poured. Close it with the one-holed stopper by fitting it with a bent glass tube.
4. Connect the bent tube to a test tube having limewater through a one-holed stopper.

*Experimental set-up 2*

Leave the two experimental set-ups undisturbed for 15–20 minutes. Make sure that the bent tube is immersed in limewater in both the cases.

**Observation:** In both the experimental set-ups, limewater gradually turns whitish in colour.

**Conclusion:** In experimental set-up 1, the germinating seeds are kept in an aerobic condition. The limewater turning whitish in colour is an indication of the release of carbon dioxide. In the experimental set-up 2, the yeast cells are kept in an anaerobic condition, but still the limewater turns whitish in colour. This is because yeast cells are capable of respiring even in anaerobic conditions.

## QUICK REVISION

**Fill in the blanks.**

1. Respiration that takes place in the presence of oxygen is called ______________.
2. Respiration that takes place in the absence of oxygen is called ______________.
3. During vigorous exercise, muscle cells break down glucose into ______________.
4. The abbreviation ATP stands for ______________.
5. The process responsible for fluffiness of bread is ______________.

## RESPIRATION IN PLANTS

Plants also respire by taking in oxygen and giving out carbon dioxide. Some structures in plants that help in respiration are mentioned below.

**Stomata:** Stomata bring about the exchange of oxygen and carbon dioxide in plant cells.

**Lenticels:** Lenticels are openings found on the barks of trees (Fig. 4.4) or stems and roots of plants. They help in the exchange of gases between the plant and the atmosphere. They can be raised, circular, oval or elongated. Even some fruits such as apples and vegetables such as potatoes have lenticels on them.

*Fig. 4.4 Lenticels on Paper Birch*

**Pneumatophores:** Pneumatophores or breathing roots are an adaptation of roots in trees usually found in mangroves in swampy areas. These trees are partially submerged, which makes gaseous exchange difficult. These roots come up from the submerged main roots in the water. They have lenticels on the surface for breathing.

## DIFFERENCES BETWEEN PHOTOSYNTHESIS AND RESPIRATION

Photosynthesis takes place only during the day because the process needs sunlight.

Respiration in plants takes place all the time; hence, during the daytime, plants use a part of the oxygen produced during photosynthesis for respiration. This oxygen is used to break down complex food materials and produce energy and carbon dioxide.

The amount of carbon dioxide produced due to respiration is not sufficient for photosynthesis, and hence, carbon dioxide is absorbed from the atmosphere. Table 4.2 gives the differences between respiration and photosynthesis.

**Table 4.2 Differences between respiration and photosynthesis**

| Respiration | Photosynthesis |
|---|---|
| It is one of the characteristic features of living things. | Green plants use this process to prepare their own food. |
| It takes place in the cells of plants, animals, human beings and microorganisms. | It takes place in the cells of plants that contain chlorophyll. |
| Oxygen is absorbed to break down the complex food that is consumed. | Oxygen is released during this process. |
| Carbon dioxide is exhaled during respiration. | Carbon dioxide is required for this process. |
| Energy is obtained through the break down of the consumed food. | Sunlight is the source of energy to produce food. |

## CONCEPT MAP

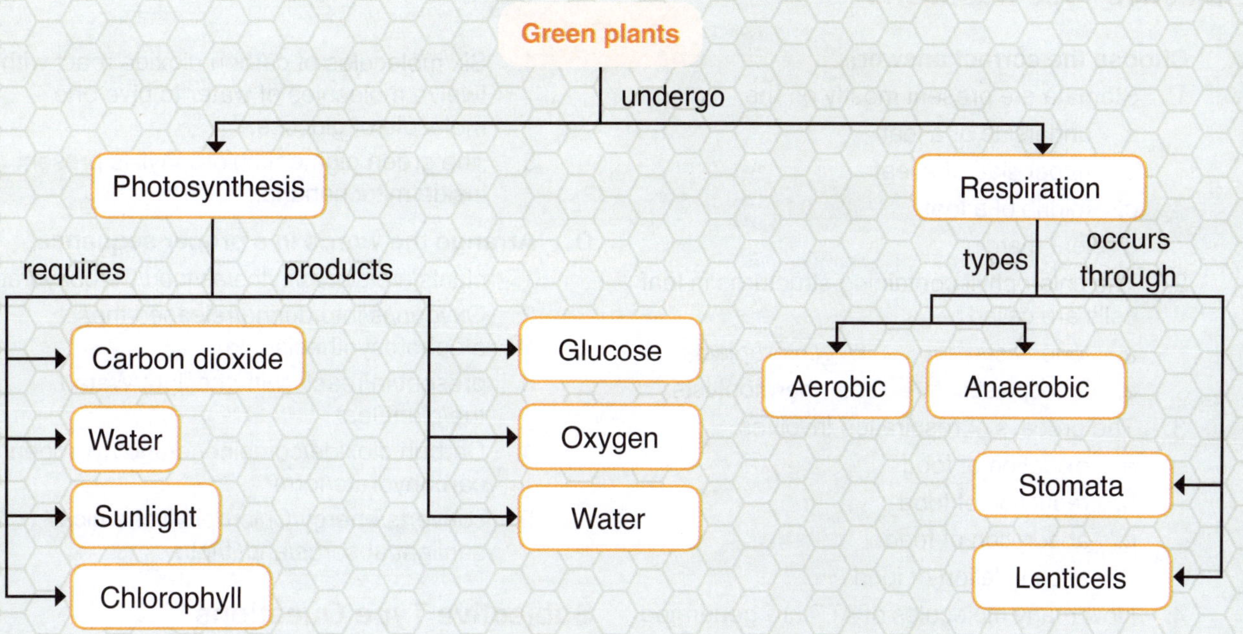


## KEYWORDS

**Photosynthesis:** the process through which plants produce food using carbon dioxide, water and sunlight in the presence of chlorophyll

**Chlorophyll:** the green pigment that helps in the absorption of sunlight

**Chloroplast:** the organelles in plant cells that contain chlorophyll

**Stomata:** the openings found mostly on the underside of leaves, through which plants take in carbon dioxide and give out oxygen

**Thylakoid:** chlorophyll-containing discs inside chloroplasts

**Grana:** stacks of thylakoids arranged inside chloroplasts

**Respiration:** the process of breaking down of food into carbon dioxide, water and energy in a living being

**ATP (adenosine triphosphate):** a chemical substance (called the **energy currency** of a cell) released during respiration

**Aerobic respiration:** a type of respiration that takes place in the presence of oxygen

**Anaerobic respiration:** a type of respiration that takes place in the absence of or in insufficient oxygen

**Lenticels:** openings found on the barks of trees or stems and roots of plants that help in the exchange of gases between the plant and the atmosphere

# Exercise

## Objective Type Questions

**A. Choose the correct answer.**

1. Stomata are present mostly on the
   a. underside of a leaf
   b. upper side of a leaf
   c. midrib of a leaf
   d. leaf margin
2. The chlorophyll containing structures in leaf cells are called
   a. tonoplasts b. chloroplasts
   c. leucoplasts d. thermoplasts
3. The process of respiration involves
   a. oxidation of food
   b. reduction of food
   c. absorption of food
   d. accumulation of food
4. How many molecules of ATP are generated at the end of aerobic respiration involving 2 molecules of glucose?
   a. 38 ATP b. 76 ATP
   c. 19 ATP d. 12 ATP
5. Respiration in plants occurs
   a. during day time
   b. during night time
   c. in vacuum
   d. all the time

**B. Fill in the blanks.**

1. Iodine turns ______________ (blue–black/reddish brown) in the presence of starch.
2. Chlorophyll helps in the absorption of ______________ (water/light).
3. The ideal temperature for photosynthesis is between ______________ (40 and 50°C/ 20 and 30°C).
4. One of the products formed during the fermentation process is ______________ (alcohol/water).
5. ______________ (Yeast/Muscle) cells carry out aerobic respiration.

**C. Write T for True and F for False.**

1. The rate of photosynthesis increases as the intensity of light decreases.
2. Plants prepare food only in the form of starch.
3. Energy produced during respiration is stored in the form of ATP.
4. Six molecules of carbon dioxide react with twelve molecules of water to give one molecule of glucose.
5. The green pigment chlorophyll is present inside mitochondria.

**D. Arrange the words in a proper sequence.**

1. plants/are/stored/in/the/as/food/Carbohydrates
2. Oxygen/is/into/during/released/the/ air/photosynthesis
3. present/in/reacts/with/the/light/Water/ the/plant/leaf
4. Carbon dioxide/combine/to/and/hydrogen/ carbohydrate/form
5. converts/energy/Chlorophyll/chemical/ sunlight/absorbs/and/it/into

## Subjective Type Questions

**A. Define the following terms.**

1. Photosynthesis
2. Respiration
3. Aerobic respiration
4. Anaerobic respiration
5. Energy currency

**B. Differentiate between the following.**

1. Aerobic and anaerobic respiration
2. Autotrophs and heterotrophs
3. Photosynthesis and respiration

**C. Answer the following questions in brief.**

1. List the factors that affect photosynthesis.
2. Explain the importance of chlorophyll in the process of photosynthesis.
3. How is carbon dioxide taken in by plants?
4. What is the full form of ATP?
5. What is the main product of anaerobic respiration?

**D. Answer the following questions in detail.**

1. Explain the structure of a chloroplast with the help of a diagram.
2. List the materials required by a leaf to photosynthesize efficiently. How are these obtained by the plant?
3. Write the procedure to test a green leaf for the presence of starch.
4. Write a note on respiration in plants.
5. Describe an experiment to show that anaerobic respiration takes place in the absence of oxygen and aerobic respiration takes place in the presence of oxygen.

## Application-based Questions

1. What happens to a plant if a part of the bark is removed?
2. What would happen if a potted plant with underground roots is overwatered?

## Picture-based Questions

Observe the image and answer the following questions.

1. What is the kind of nutrition in this plant?
2. What are these kind of plants called?
3. Do these plant photosynthesize and respire like any other plants?
4. Why do these plants depend on small insects as one of the sources for nutrients?
5. Give two more examples of such type of plants.

# Skill Booster

**A.** **21CS:** Life Sills | **EL** | **BT:** Psychomotor

Germinate some seeds. Plant them in a tray with soil mixed with humus. Sprinkle water to add moisture to the plantlets regularly. Observe the tiny root hairs that develop after a week.

**B.** **21CS:** Critical Thinking, Information Literacy | **AI** | **BT:** Cognitive, Psychomotor

Have you seen plants that have yellow- or red-coloured leaves? Why do you think these plants have such colours? Find out the names of two such plants and the reason why they have such colours. Collect fallen leaves of such plants and create a herbarium. Add information based on your findings.

# Worksheet 4

A community has a very lush and green park. Residents spend their leisure time and play in this park. However, authorities are finding it difficult to maintain this area. They are planning to cut down some trees. Majority of the people in the community are against it and have asked the authorities to think of alternative ways to take care of the area.

It so happened that a similar community chopped down the trees. Now, they are finding it difficult to bear the heat. Many residents in that community were also diagnosed with certain health issues.

## My SEE Journal

A. Was the decision of finding new ways to tackle the situation a small step towards the improvement of global environment development? What would be your suggestion to overcome this situation?

_______________________________________________

_______________________________________________

_______________________________________________

_______________________________________________

_______________________________________________

B. How do plants and trees contribue to the global environment?

_______________________________________________

_______________________________________________

_______________________________________________

## My SDG Journal

13 CLIMATE ACTION

Design an awareness poster explaining the importance of plants, their life processes and their role in decreasing global warming.

# 5 Excretory System and Nervous System

**Prior Knowledge**

- Life processes in animals
- Organs involved in excretory system
- Organs involved in nervous system

**Learning Objectives**

- Excretion in human beings
    - Renal excretory system
    - Disorders of the urinary system
- Human nervous system
    - Role of nervous system in control and coordination
    - Structure and function of nerve cells
    - Structure and function of the brain and spinal cord

## LET'S GET STARTED

Identify and name the organ systems given below. Which organ system do you find the most interesting to study? Give reasons for your answer.

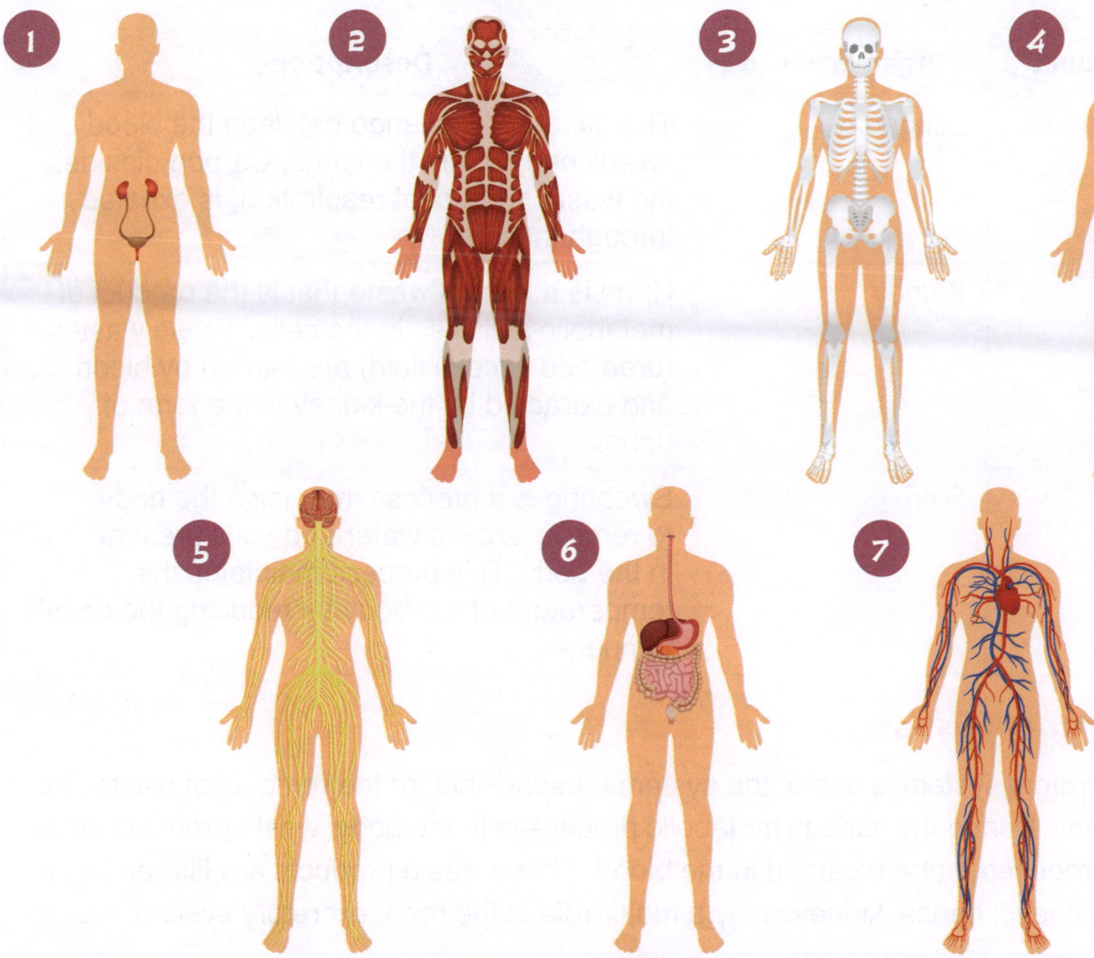

## ORGAN SYSTEMS

The human body performs many functions such as respiration, digestion and circulation. Some waste products are generated in these processes. Accumulation of wastes in the body leads to many health disorders. Therefore, these wastes need to be regularly removed from the body. The **excretory system** in humans plays an important role in removing these wastes from the body.

A change in the environment to which an organism reacts is called a **stimulus** (plural: stimuli). Stimuli can be external or internal. Light, sound, smell, pain, touch and taste are some of the external stimuli we come across in our daily life. Internal stimuli are those that come from within the organism's body. For example, hunger, thirst and sleep. The reaction of an organism to a stimulus is called a **response**. For example, if we accidentally touch a hot object, we respond by moving the hand away from that object. Our responses to internal and external stimuli are controlled by the **nervous system**.

## EXCRETION IN HUMAN BEINGS

The amount of waste products produced in the human body is higher than that in plants. Activities involving respiratory and digestive systems are the main contributors to the formation of waste products in the body. Table 5.1 gives the various ways in which these waste products are excreted.

**Table 5.1 Waste products in humans**

| Waste Product | Organ Involved | Description |
|---|---|---|
| Carbon dioxide | Lungs | The gaseous exchange between the blood and alveoli happens in the lungs. Carbon dioxide, the waste product of respiration, is exhaled through the nose. |
| Urine | Kidney | Urine is a human waste that is the product of metabolic activities in the cells. These wastes (urea and excess fluid) are carried by blood and extracted by the kidney in the form of urine. |
| Sweat | Skin | Sweating is a process that helps the body to remove excess water and salts present in the body. This process maintains the temperature of the body by reducing the body's temperature. |

### Renal Excretory System

The renal excretory system is one of the systems responsible for the removal of wastes from the human body. During the various metabolic processes in the body, waste products such as urea are produced that are carried in the blood. These waste products are filtered from the blood in kidneys; hence, kidneys play a major role in the renal excretory system.

The kidneys are aided by other organs such as the ureter, urinary bladder and urethra (Fig. 5.1).

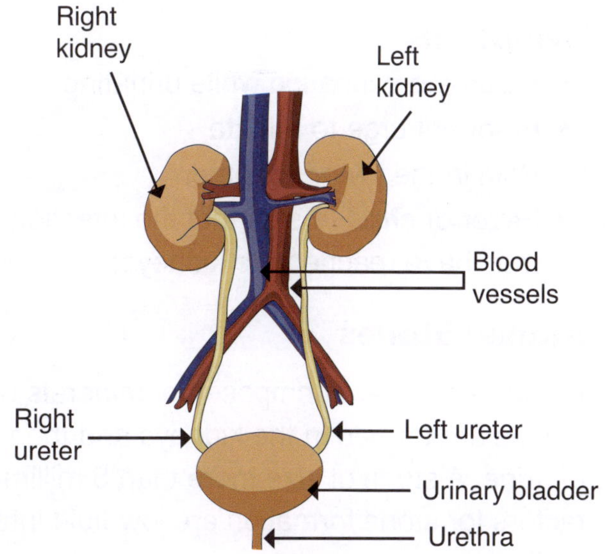


*Fig. 5.1 Renal excretory system*

**Kidneys**: Kidneys are brownish, bean-shaped organs, placed on either sides of the spinal cord or the backbone. A kidney is approximately 4 inches in length and 2 inches in width. Each kidney (Fig. 5.2) is connected with blood vessels that carry blood with the waste products in them. Another blood vessel is connected to take away the blood that is free of waste products.

The longitudinal section of a kidney shows an outer region called **cortex** and an inner region called **medulla**.

Kidneys have a network of coiled tubes called **nephrons** that filter out wastes from the blood. Nephrons are called the structural and functional units of the kidneys.

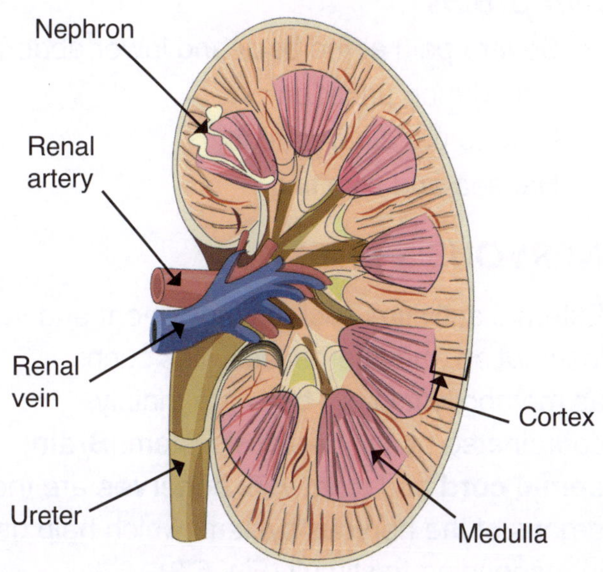


*Fig. 5.2 Structure of a kidney*

**Ureter:** A ureter is connected to each kidney. The tubules of the nephrons carry the wastes to the ureter. From the ureter, the urine moves into the urinary bladder.

**Urinary Bladder:** It is a sac that stores the urine for a short period of time. It is connected to the two ureters.

**Urethra:** It is the passage that moves the urine out of the urinary bladder and out of the body.

## DISORDERS OF THE URINARY SYSTEM

Urinary system disorders affect the organs of the urinary system: kidneys, urinary bladder and ureters. Urinary tract infections (UTIs), kidney stones and kidney failure are the common urinary disorders.

### Urinary Tract Infection (UTI)

These infections affect the upper part (kidney infection) or lower part of the urinary tract (bladder infection). The most common causative microorganism is *Escherichia coli.* It enters the bladder through the urethra and multiplies. Women are more prone to UTIs because of their anatomy.

### *Symptoms*

- A burning sensation while urinating
- Frequent urge to urinate
- Pain in the lower abdomen
- Fever or chills (a sign that the infection may have reached the kidneys)

### *Prevention and Treatment*

- Maintaining personal hygiene
- Drink plenty of water
- UTIs are usually treated with antibiotics

## Kidney Stones

Kidney stones are composed of minerals or salts found in the urinary tract. Usually, these stones are formed in the kidneys and then pass into the urinary tract through the stream of urine. A stone of size more than 5 millimetres can cause blockage in ureters. The major factors for stone formation are low fluid intake and high intake of animal protein, sugars and sodium.

### *Symptoms*

- Severe pain at the back and lower abdomen
- Pain during urination
- Urge to urinate frequently
- Nausea and vomiting

### *Prevention and Treatment*

- Drinking plenty of water
- Avoiding high protein, sugar or salt diet
- Medication to relieve pain
- Medical procedures to remove stones

# NERVOUS SYSTEM

External activities such as movement and locomotion and internal activities such as metabolism in our body are mainly coordinated by the nervous system. **Brain**, **spinal cord** and a network of **nerves** are the organs of the nervous system, which help us in responding to stimuli (Fig. 5.3).

Our **sense organs** such as eyes, ears, nose, skin and tongue help in detecting stimuli. Messages from our sense organs are taken to the brain by the nerves. This is similar to electrical signals being passed through electrical wires.

The messages passed through the nervous system are called **nerve impulses**. The brain also sends nerve impulses in return to the stimuli to muscles and glands of the body, which show the response.

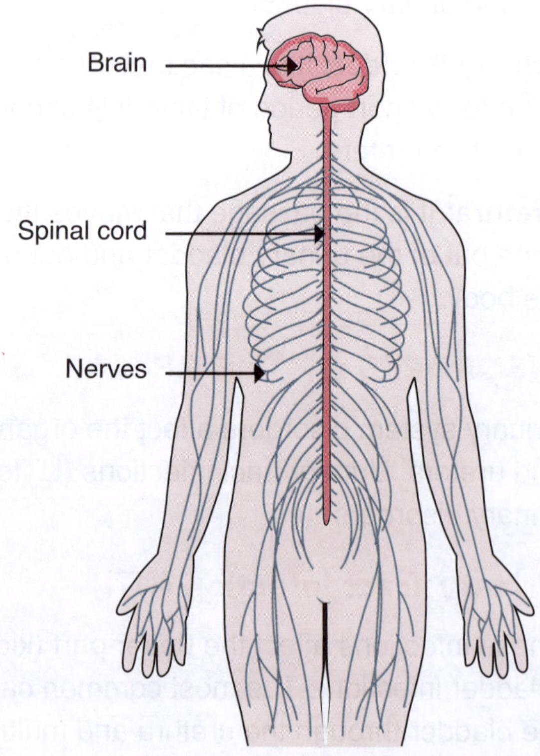

*Fig. 5.3 Nervous system*

## Nerves

Nerve cells are the basic unit of the nervous system. A nerve cell is also called **neuron**.

### *Structure of a Neuron*

Figure 5.4 shows the structure of a neuron. A neuron contains a nucleus and the cell body (cyton) extends to form branched structures called **dendrons**. Dendrons branch out further into structures called **dendrites**. One of the dendrites elongates from the cell body to form a tail-like structure called **axon**.

Axon is insulated and protected by a sheath-like structure called **myelin sheath**. The myelin sheath is discontinuous at certain places. These places are called **nodes of Ranvier**. The junction between two neurons (the dendrite of one neuron and the axon terminal of another) is called a **synapse**.

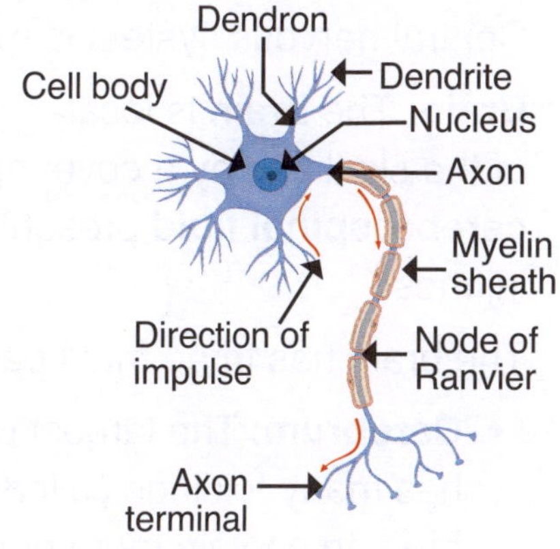

*Fig. 5.4 Neuron*

Functions of dendrites, axon and myelin sheath are:

- The messages or nerve impulses are received by the dendrites.
- The axon transmits the nerve impulses to different neurons, muscles and glands.
- The myelin sheath insulates the axon and increases the rate of transmission of nerve signals or impulse.

Nerve impulses pass at a speed of 100 metres per second. A nerve can, however, conduct about 1000 nerve impulses each second.

### *Types of Neurons*

There are three types of neurons: sensory, motor and interneuron.

- **Sensory or afferent neuron:** These neurons carry nerve impulses from the sense organs to the brain or spinal cord [Fig. 5.5 (a)].
- **Motor or efferent neuron:** These neurons [Fig. 5.5 (b)] carry nerve impulses from the spinal cord or brain to the muscles or glands. Motor neurons are connected to the muscles at junctions called the **neuromuscular junction**.
- **Interneuron or association neuron:** Afferent neuron and efferent neuron are connected by interneurons [Fig. 5.5 (c)].

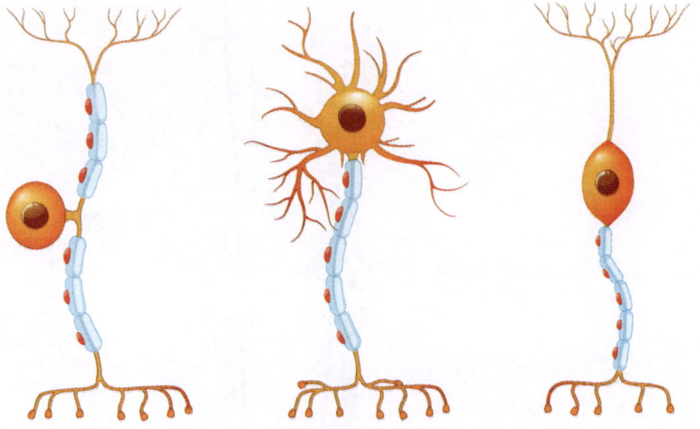
(a) Sensory neuron (b) Motor neuron (c) Interneuron

*Fig. 5.5 Types of nerve cells*

## Human Nervous System

The human nervous system (Fig. 5.6) can be divided into central nervous system and peripheral nervous system.

### *Central Nervous System*

Central nervous system is made up of the brain and the spinal cord.

**Brain:** The **brain** is located in the head inside the skull. The brain is protected by the bones of the skull and by a covering of three thin membranes called **meninges**. A fluid called **cerebrospinal fluid** present between the meninges protects the brain from shocks and injuries.

The brain has three main parts: cerebrum, cerebellum and brainstem.

- **Cerebrum:** The largest part of the brain is known as cerebrum. The surface of cerebrum has many foldings called **furrows** and **ridges**, which increase the surface area of the brain to contain more nerve cells.

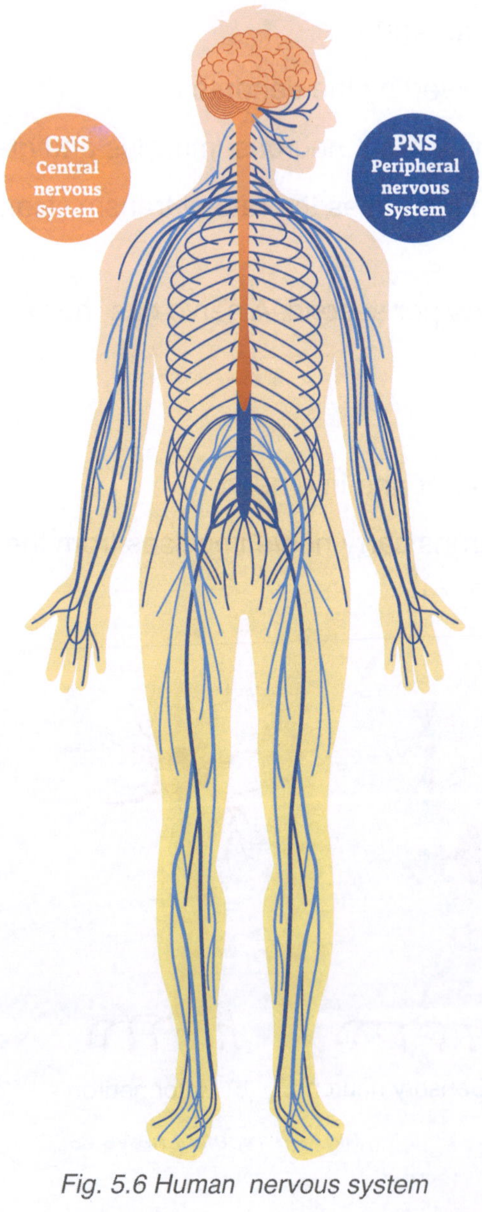


*Fig. 5.6 Human nervous system*

**TECH INFO**

Magnetic resonance imaging (MRI) is a technique used to identify the response of different parts of the brain to external stimuli.

The cerebrum is divided into left and right **cerebral hemispheres** with a deep furrow between them [Fig. 5.7 (a)]. Memory, intelligence, reasoning and other mental activities including response to stimuli are controlled by the cerebrum.

- **Cerebellum:** It is located below the cerebrum [Fig. 5.7 (b)]. This part of the brain controls and coordinates muscular movements of the body and also maintains the balance of the body.
- **Brainstem:** It connects the brain to the spinal cord. The brainstem consists of three parts: midbrain, pons and medulla oblongata.
    - o **Midbrain:** It is the top part of the brainstem. It helps in regulating eye movements.
    - o **Pons:** It is the middle portion of the brainstem. It coordinates facial movements, hearing and balance.
    - o **Medulla oblongata:** It is the bottom part of the brainstem. It helps in regulating our breathing, heart rhythms, blood pressure and swallowing.

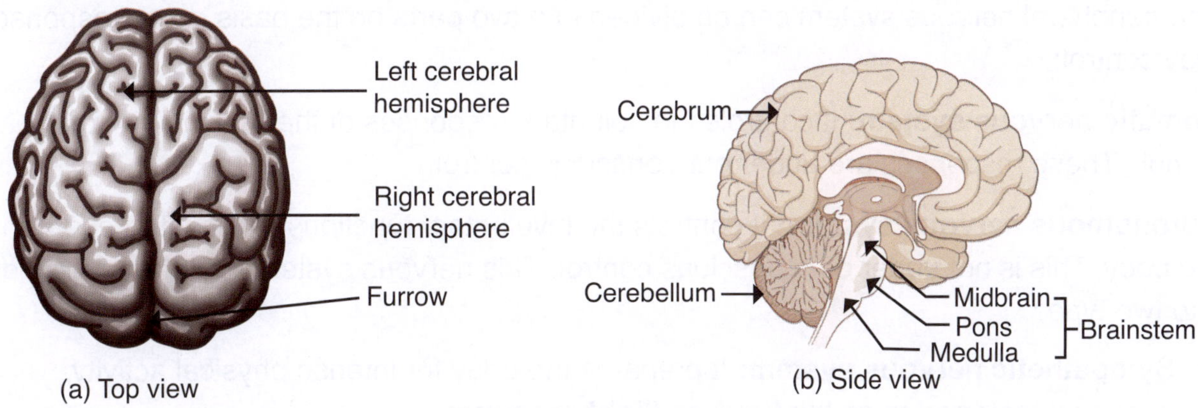


*Fig. 5.7 Human brain*

**Spinal cord:** Spinal cord is the continuation of the brainstem. It is found inside the vertebral column [Fig. 5.8 (a) and (b)].

A cross-section of the spinal cord [Fig. 5.8 (c)] looks like a butterfly with a canal-like structure in the middle. This canal is known as the **central canal**. It contains cerebrospinal fluid. It is surrounded by an H-shaped area called the **grey matter**, made up of cell bodies of the neurons. The outer area surrounding the grey matter is called **white matter**. It is made up of nerve fibres.

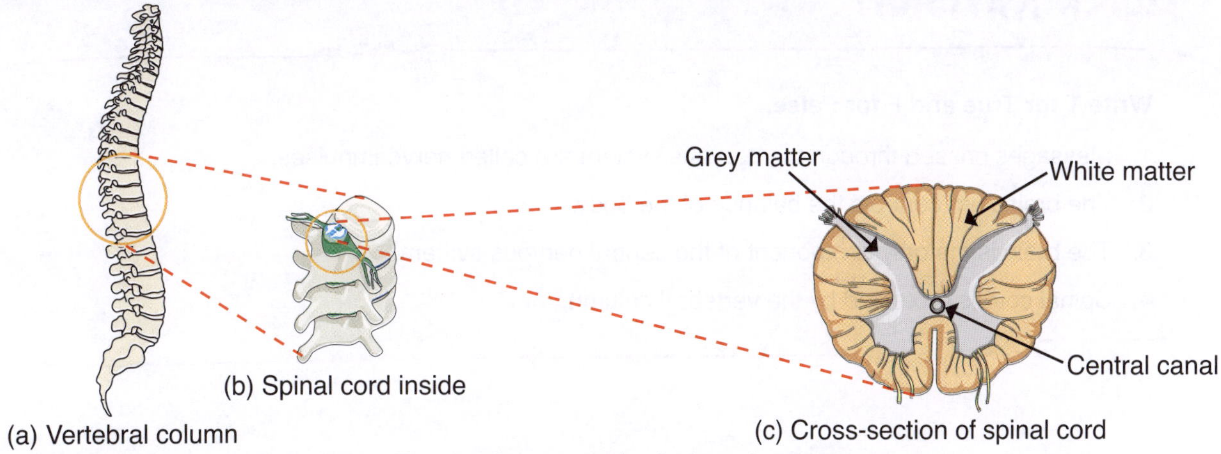


*Fig. 5.8 Structure of spinal cord*

The main functions of the spinal cord are given below.

- It carries nerve signals throughout our body.
- It transmits impulses from the organs of the body to the brain and from the brain to the other body parts.
- It controls some reflexes without involving the brain.

## *Peripheral Nervous System*

The peripheral nervous system consists of the cranial and spinal nerves.

The nerves that arise from the brain are called **cranial nerves**. There are 12 pairs of cranial nerves that are involved in transmission of both sensory and motor signals.

**Spinal nerves** originate from the spinal cord. There are 31 pairs of spinal nerves. They carry nerve impulses to and from the spinal cord to the other parts of the body.

The peripheral nervous system can be divided into two parts on the basis of the responses they control:

**Somatic nervous system:** It controls the voluntary responses of the body to external stimuli. These responses are under our conscious control.

**Autonomous nervous system:** It controls the involuntary functions of the internal organs of the body. This is not under our conscious control. This nervous system is further subdivided into two types:

- **Sympathetic nervous system:** It prepares the body for intense physical activity, commonly referred to as the **fight-or-flight response**.
- **Parasympathetic nervous system:** It relaxes the body and slows down many functions that require more energy, commonly called the **rest-and-digest response**.

  Both these systems control the same group of body functions, but they have opposite effects on the functions they regulate. For example, the sympathetic nervous system increases heart rate, whereas parasympathetic nervous system slows it down.

## QUICK REVISION

**Write T for True and F for False.**

1. Messages passed through the nervous system are called nerve impulses.
2. The brainstem controls the balance of the body.
3. The brain is the only component of the central nervous system.
4. Spinal cord is protected by the vertebral column.

## CONCEPT MAP

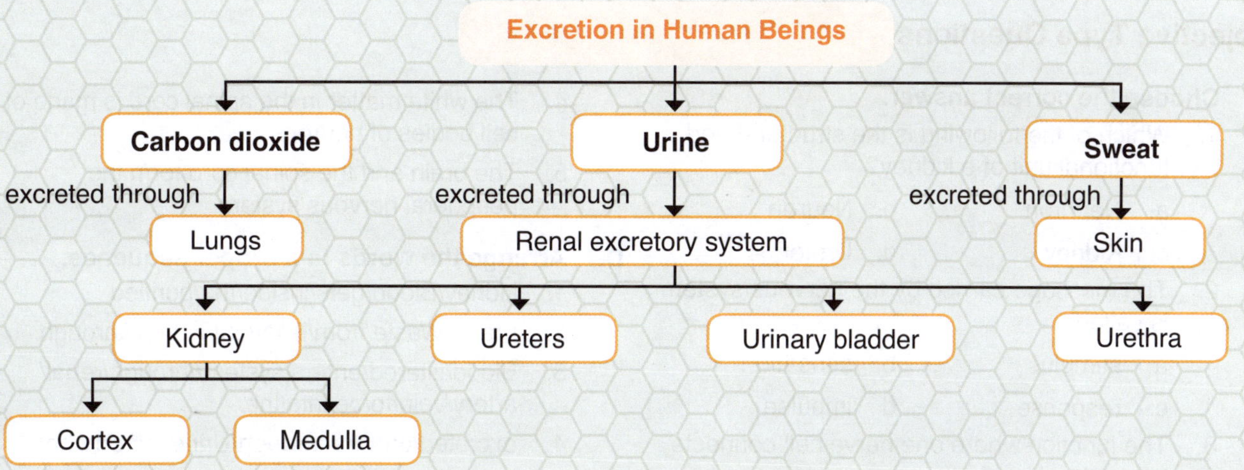


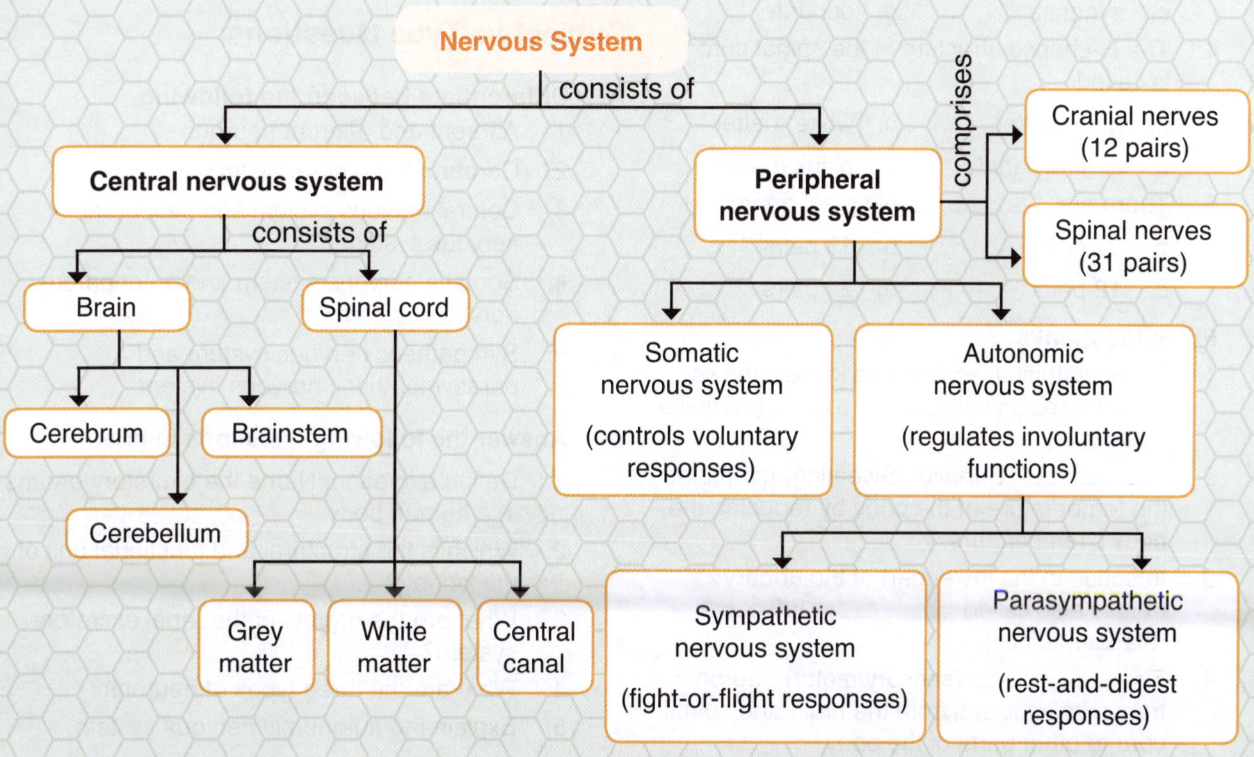


## KEYWORDS

**Excretion:** the removal of waste products produced due to life processes from the body

**Dendrite:** the branched structures arising from the cell body of a neuron

**Myelin sheath:** a layer of insulation around the axon of a neuron

**Nerve impulse:** the messages passed through the nervous system

**Meninges:** protective layers located between the brain and the skull

# Exercise

## Objective Type Questions

**A. Choose the correct answer.**

1. Which of the following is the structural and functional unit of a kidney?
   a. Nephron  b. Neuron
   c. Kidney  d. Ureter
2. The message carried by the nervous system is called
   a. stimulus  b. sensation
   c. response  d. impulse
3. The junction where one nerve cell connects to another is called
   a. axon  b. dendron
   c. synapse  d. dendrite
4. The H-shaped structure in the spinal cord is called
   a. grey matter  b. white matter
   c. central canal  d. black matter
5. There are __________ of spinal nerves.
   a. 31 pairs  b. 13 pairs
   c. 12 pairs  d. 24 pairs

**B. Fill in the blanks.**

1. The longitudinal section of a kidney shows an outer region called __________ (medulla/cortex)
2. __________ (Urination/Sweating) maintains the temperature of the body by reducing the body's temperature.
3. Infection in the lower part of the urinary tract is also called __________ infection (bladder/kidney).
4. The __________ (sensory/motor) neuron transmits impulses from the brain and spinal cord to other parts of the body.
5. The __________ (somatic/autonomous) nervous system controls the voluntary responses of the body to external stimuli.

**C. Write T for True and F for False.**

1. Urine and sweat are the only two waste products formed in the human body.
2. Axon is insulated and protected by the nodes of Ranvier.
3. Afferent and efferent neurons are connected by interneurons.
4. The white matter in the spinal cord is made of cell bodies of neurons.
5. The brain and the spinal cord form the peripheral nervous system.

**D. Arrange the words in a proper sequence.**

1. kidney/Blood/gets/inside/the/purified
2. ureter/Waste/from/is/let/out/kidney/through
3. Blood/filtered/enters/system/through/renal/artery/vein/to/be/into/the
4. excreted/urethra/through/Urine/is/from/the/body
5. stores/bladder/the/urine/Urinary

## Subjective Type Questions

**A. Differentiate between the following.**

1. Afferent and efferent neurons
2. Cerebrum and cerebellum
3. Central nervous system and peripheral nervous system
4. Somatic nervous system and autonomous nervous system
5. Sympathetic nervous system and parasympathetic nervous system

**B. Answer the following questions in brief.**

1. Define excretion. Name the excretory organs in a human body.
2. Which is the structural and functional unit of the kidney?
3. What are the organs of the renal excretory system?
4. What are the three types of neurons?
5. Explain the autonomic nervous system.

**C. Answer the following questions in detail.**

1. Describe the renal excretory system with the help of a diagram.
2. Describe the structure of a human kidney.
3. What are the common excretory disorders found in human? Explain.
4. Write a note on the human brain, its structure and functions.
5. Describe the peripheral nervous system.

## Application-based Question

What would happen to a living organism if it did not get rid of wastes from its body?

## Picture-based Questions

Observe the images and answer the following questions.

1. In which part of the nerve cell do we see a nucleus?
2. Which part of the brain controls the right side of our body?
3. Which is the most common neurotransmitter seen in the synapse region of a nerve cell?
4. Does cerebral palsy affect the whole body? Which body part does it affect?
5. Which part of the nerve receives the nerve impulse?

a.

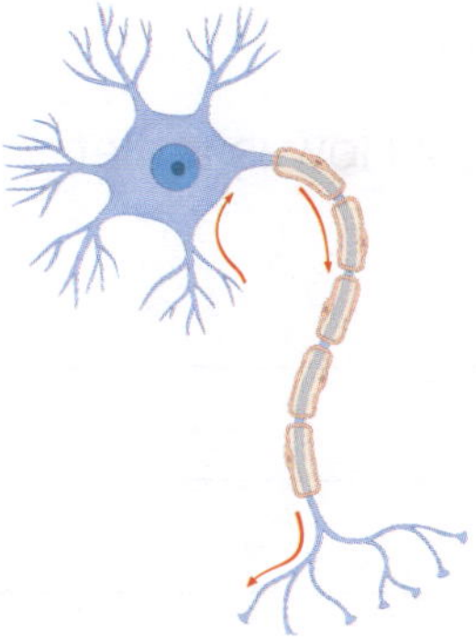

b.

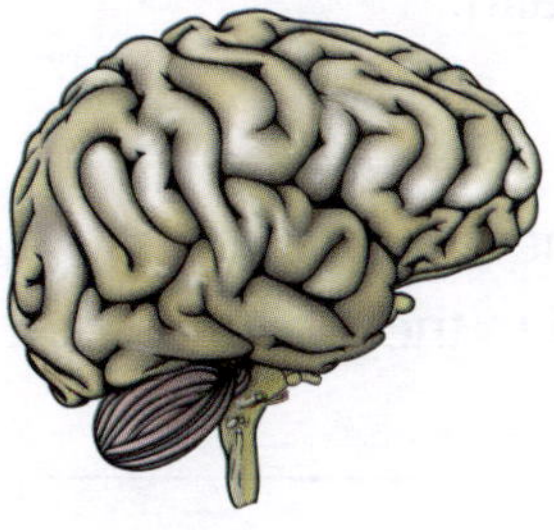

# Skill Booster

**A.** **21CS:** Communication, Creativity and Innovation | **EL** | **BT:** Psychomotor

Prepare a model of human excretory system with biodegradable materials and display it in the class.

**B.** **21CS:** Information Literacy, Communication | **BT:** Cognitive, Affective

Refer your library books and make a report on any three neurological disorders such as epilepsy, seizures and dementia. Create a poster to spread awareness about these disorders.

**C.** **21CS:** Creativity and Innovation | **AI** | **BT:** Psychomotor

Make a model of the human brain using clay or play dough.

**D.** **21CS:** Information Literacy | **BT:** Affective

Find out which skills are associated with the left and right parts of the brain. Analyze your own skills. Which part of your brain do you think is more developed?

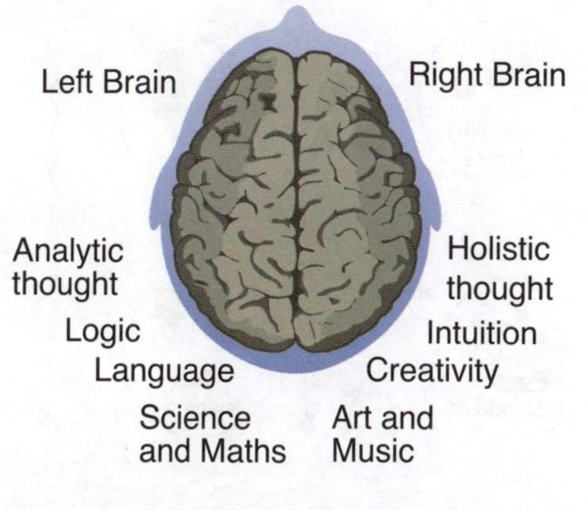

# Worksheet 5

James was a very active student in his class. Post pandemic, he became very weak and had constant tingling in the nerve ends and muscle weakness. His teachers noticed that his concentration level was also depreciating gradually.

His parents consulted with a doctor. The doctor diagnosed that James was running short of certain vitamins in his system. He was suggested to include vitamin B-rich food in his diet to improve his health.

## My SEE Journal

A. Why did the doctor suggest James to have vitamin B-rich food? How is a diet connected to the wellness of the nervous system?

B. What would have happened if the change in James' behaviour was noticed and he wasn't taken to see a specialist?

## My SDG Journal

3 GOOD HEALTH AND WELL-BEING

It is essential to maintain the health of kidneys to have an efficiently functioning excretory system. Mrs X here is shown having certain habits. Observe the image and list the 'Don'ts' she should follow to have a healthy excretory system.

# 6 Health and Hygiene: Allergy

**Prior Knowledge**

- Definition of health
- Balanced diet
- Importance of health

**Learning Objectives**

- Allergy and allergens
- Symptoms produced by allergens
- Seasonal or perennial allergy
- Precautions to be taken for allergy

## LET'S GET STARTED

In recent days, we all have witnessed the COVID-19 pandemic and have realized the importance of hygiene.

List the hygiene practices that have helped us during the pandemic.

1

2

3

4

5

Our body defends itself against infections and other harmful invaders such as bacteria and viruses with the help of our immune system. We would constantly fall sick from bacteria, viruses or other foreign substances without our immune system. Our immune system is made up of different organs, cells and proteins that work together.

## COMMON ALLERGENS AND THEIR ENTRY ROUTES

Hypersensitive immune response to substances that either enter or come in contact with the body is called an **allergy**. It occurs when one's immune system reacts to a substance in the environment. The substances that cause an allergic reaction are called **allergens**.

Some examples of allergens are dust mites, pollen, strong sunlight, food items, moulds and some medicines.

> **DO YOU KNOW?**
>
> A substance that is an allergen to one person may not be an allergen to another.

### Dust Mites

Dust mites are the most common cause of allergy from dust. They live and multiply in warm and humid places. Dust mites are a common cause of asthma in children. They float into air when someone vacuums, walks on a carpet or disturbs a bedding, and they settle once the disturbance is over.

The nose and the mouth are the common entry routes of dust mites.

### Pollen Grains

Pollens are fine to coarse powdery substance consisting of pollen grains, which are the male gametes produced by trees, grasses, flowers and weeds. People can be allergic to different types of pollen (Fig. 6.1). For example, some people are allergic to pollen from only beech trees; while a few are allergic to pollen from grasses.

The nose and the mouth are the common entry routes of this allergen.

### Strong Sunlight

Itchy red rashes occur on the skin when exposed to sunlight; this condition is often known as **sun allergy** (Fig. 6.2). Polymorphic light eruption (PLE) is the most common form of sun allergy. It is also known as sun poisoning. In PLE, when light hits the skin, it causes slight changes in the skin cells and the individual's body reacts against these changes to fight them off. This causes itchy spots or blisters.

The skin is the only route for the entry of this allergen.

*Fig. 6.1 Pollen grains*

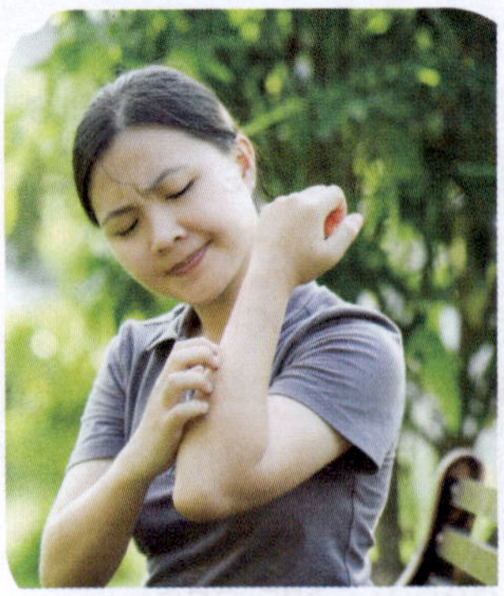

*Fig. 6.2 Itchy hands*

## Food Items

Fig. 6.3 Food allergens

Some food items that account for about 90 per cent of the allergic reactions are eggs, milk, peanuts, tree nuts (almonds, cashews, walnuts, etc.), fish, shellfish, wheat, soy, sesame and mustard seeds (Fig. 6.3). Symptoms may involve the skin, the gastrointestinal tract, the cardiovascular system and the respiratory tract.

A type of delayed food allergy reaction seen in infants is food protein-induced enterocolitis syndrome (FPIES). It is a severe gastrointestinal reaction that generally occurs two to six hours after consuming milk, soy or certain grains.

This allergen enters into the body through the mouth.

# SYMPTOMS OF AN ALLERGIC REACTION

When an allergic person comes in contact with an allergen, an allergic reaction occurs. When the allergens enter the body, a response gets triggered by the release of certain chemical substances called histamines. This results in swelling and inflammation, which is extremely irritating and uncomfortable.

Some symptoms commonly triggered by different categories of allergens are given below:

- Allergens that enter through the skin trigger symptoms such as eczema and hives (Fig. 6.4), and those that enter into the lungs cause asthma.
- Allergens that enter from the nose and/or eyes trigger symptoms such as conjunctivitis (Fig. 6.5, inflammation of the eyes that cause the eyes to become red and watery) and allergic rhinitis (inflammation of the mucous membrane that lines the nose).
- Food allergens trigger symptoms such as vomiting and/or stomach cramps, shortness of breath, wheezing, repetitive cough, hoarse throat, swelling of the tongue and lips (Fig. 6.6), pale or blue colouring of skin, dizziness or feeling faint, and anaphylaxis.

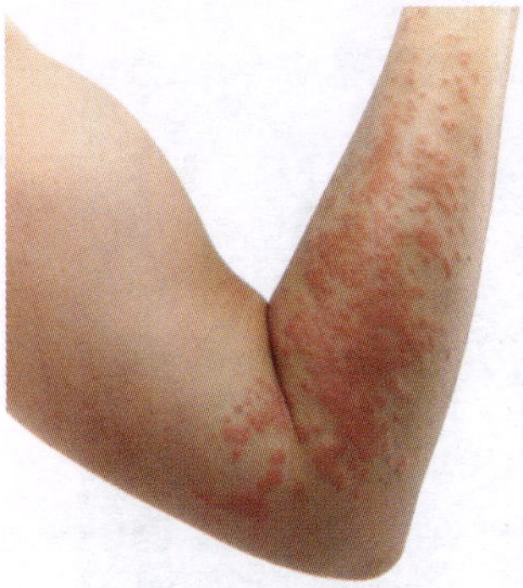

Fig. 6.4 Hives

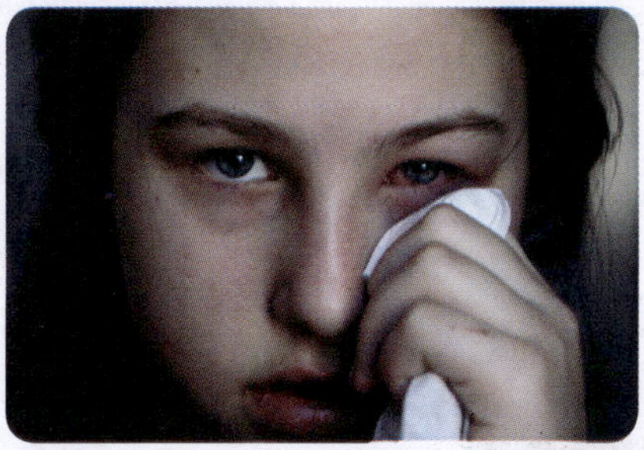

Fig. 6.5 Conjunctivitis

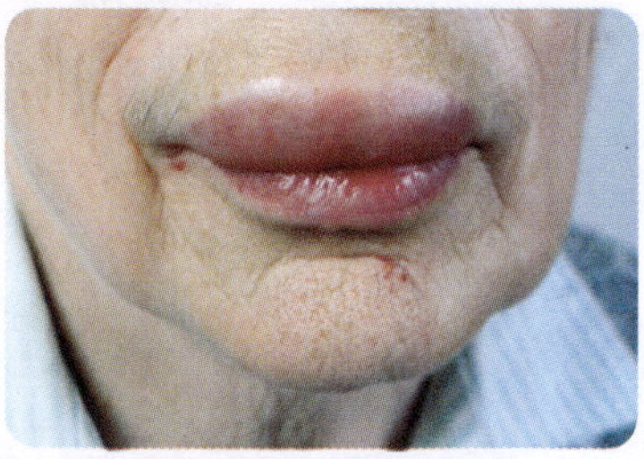

Fig. 6.6 Swollen lips

## QUICK REVISION

**Match the following.**

| | | | |
|---|---|---|---|
| 1. | Peanuts | a. | Male gametes from flowers |
| 2. | Polymorphic light eruption | b. | Delayed food allergy in infants |
| 3. | Dust mites | c. | Food allergen |
| 4. | Food protein-induced enterocolitis syndrome | d. | Asthma in children |
| 5. | Pollens | e. | Sun allergy |

## TYPES OF ALLERGY

Allergies can be categorized into the following types:

- **Non-seasonal** or **perennial allergy** can occur any time of a year. Dust, dust mites, dander (small particles or scales of hair or feathers, dandruff, etc.), saliva from dogs and cats and moulds (Fig. 6.7) are some common perennial allergens.
- **Seasonal allergy** occurs at a particular time every year. This type of allergy usually occurs during the season when the pollen from plants is dispersed. Trees (especially in the spring), grasses, plants such as hay, wheat and corn (mostly present in the summer), and herbaceous plants during the end of summer and in fall (ragweed, Fig. 6.8) are some of the common seasonal allergens. Seasonal allergy due to pollens is also called **hay fever**. Symptoms of hay fever include sneezing, runny nose and watery eyes due to inflammation of the mucous membranes of the eyes and nose.

  Another form of seasonal allergy is caused during the rainy season due to the spores released by moulds.

### DO YOU KNOW?

Not everyone who experiences symptoms after eating certain food items has food allergy. For example, some people experience an itchy mouth and throat after eating a raw or uncooked fruit or vegetable. This may indicate oral allergy syndrome – a reaction to pollen, not to the food.

*Fig. 6.7 Moulds growing on old buildings*

*Fig. 6.8 Ragweed*

## PRECAUTIONS AND CARE

Some of the precautions and care to be taken by a person prone to allergies are given in Table 6.1.

**Table 6.1 Allergies: Precautions and care**

| Allergies | Precautions and Care |
|---|---|
| Dust allergy | • Get rid of carpets and dust-collecting furniture such as stuffed chairs, periodically.<br>• Wash sheets, pillow cases and bedspreads in hot water.<br>• Clean floors regularly.<br>• Keep the ambient humidity level low.<br>• Install a high-efficiency air filter.<br>• Go for allergy shots if the allergy persists for a long time. |
| Pollen allergy | • Keep doors and windows closed.<br>• Do not mow the lawn or go to places where your allergen can be found (e.g. parks and other areas with plants).<br>• Do not dry your clothes on the clothesline.<br>• Wear sunglasses whenever you are outside.<br>• Control some symptoms with over-the-counter medication such as decongestants and antihistamines (eye drops, nasal spray and oral medication).<br>• Consult an allergist for prescription medications. |
| Skin allergy | • Always cover the body before going out in the sun.<br>• Apply sunscreen lotions on the exposed parts of the body before going out.<br>• Consult an allergist immediately in case of any itch or blister. |
| Food allergy | • Be extra careful when eating in restaurants.<br>• Epinephrine (adrenaline) is the first-line treatment for anaphylaxis.<br>• Consult a doctor for treatment. |

**Anaphylaxis:** Anaphylaxis is a severe allergic reaction that can arise within minutes of exposure to an allergen to which a person might have been exposed once before. This is a condition where the breathing/heart rate of an individual is impaired by a sudden drop in blood pressure. It can be fatal if not treated at the earliest.

## CONCEPT MAP

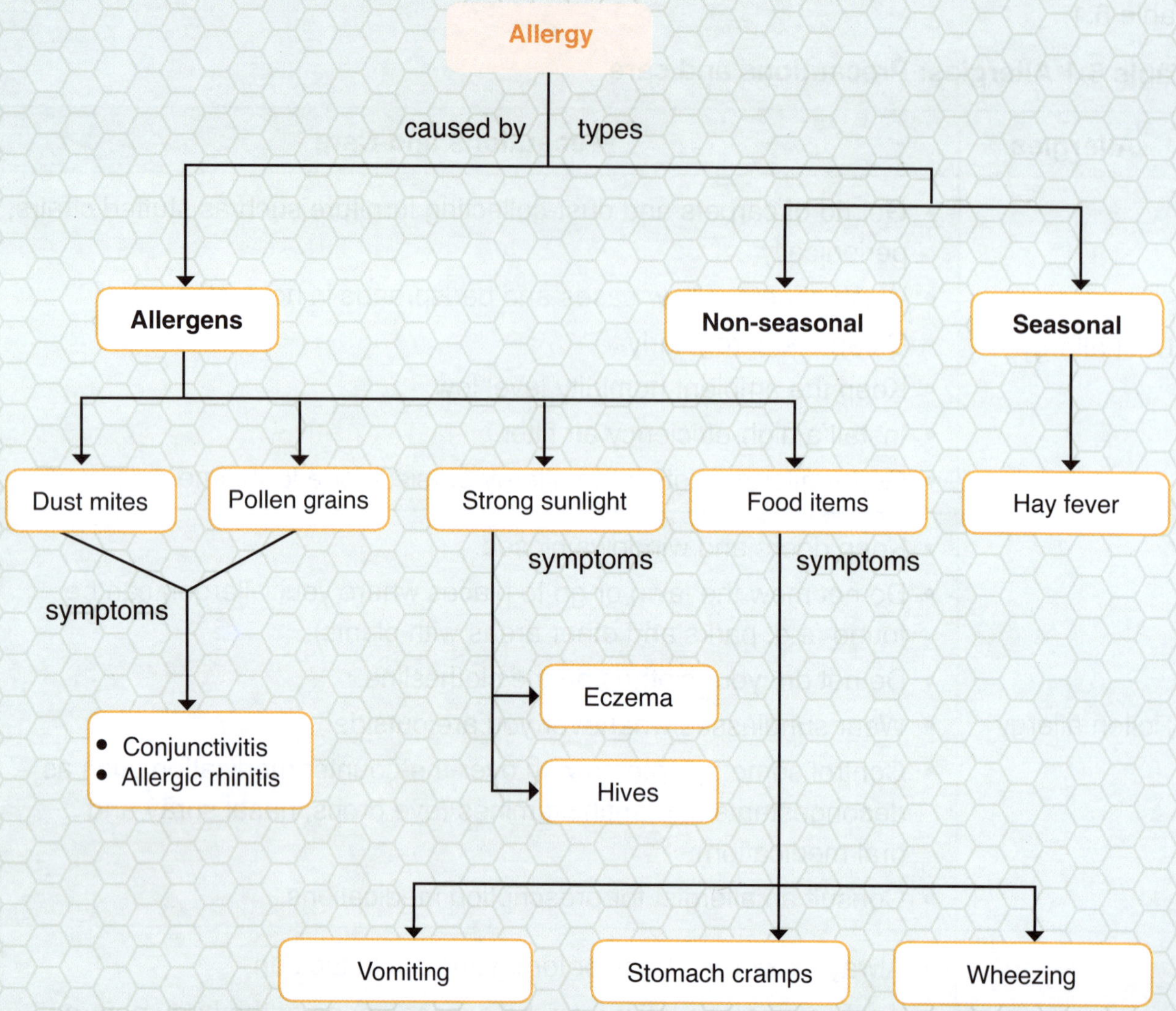


## KEYWORDS

**Allergy:** a hypersensitive response of the body to certain substances
**Allergen:** any substance that causes allergy
**Pollen:** a fine coarse powdery substance consisting of pollen grains
**Conjunctivitis:** an inflammation of the conjunctiva of the eye
**Allergic rhinitis:** an inflammation in the nose in response to an allergen
**Anaphylaxis:** an acute allergic hypersensitive reaction to an allergen
**Perennial allergy:** an allergy that can occur through the year
**Seasonal allergy:** an allergy that occurs at the same time every year

# Exercise

## Objective Type Questions

**A. Choose the correct answer.**

1. Which of these causes polymorphic light eruption?
   a. Pollen grains  b. Dust mites
   c. Soya milk  d. Sunlight
2. Food protein-induced enterocolitis syndrome shows symptoms in the ______.
   a. gastrointestinal tract
   b. respiratory tract
   c. circulatory tract
   d. cardiovascular system
3. Which of these cause food allergy?
   a. Weeds  b. Grasses
   c. Mites  d. Fish
4. Eczema and hives are the symptoms seen in which of these organs?
   a. Skin  b. Eyes
   c. Stomach  d. Lungs
5. Which of these is not a symptom of food allergy?
   a. Vomiting
   b. Pale colouring of skin
   c. Anaphylaxis
   d. Asthma

**B. Fill in the blanks.**

1. Ragweed causes ______________ allergy. (seasonal/perennial)
2. Epinephrine is the first line of treatment for ______________. (asthma/anaphylaxis)
3. Pollen allergy can be controlled by ______________, an over-the-counter medicine. (antihistamine/adrenaline)
4. Asthma in children is caused by ___________. (pollen grains/dust mites)
5. Hypersensitive immune response to a substance is called an ______________. (allergen/allergy)

**C. Write T for true and F for False.**

1. Hay fever is also known as perennial allergy.
2. A substance that is an allergen to one person will be an allergen to all.
3. Dust mites float in the air and enter the body through the nose and mouth.
4. Peanuts and fish are the most common food allergens.
5. Polymorphic light eruption is also known as sun poisoning.

**D. Arrange the words in a proper sequence.**

1. allergy/called/Hypersensitive/is/substance/immune/response/to/any
2. allergens/Substances/that/allergic/reaction/cause/an/are/called/as
3. enters/Pollen/while/into/body/the/breathing
4. may/Peanut/be/allergen/not/to/all/an
5. prevented/Allergy/can/be/avoiding/by/the/allergens

## Subjective Type Questions

**A. Define the following terms.**

1. Allergy
2. Allergens
3. Polymorphic light eruption
4. Anaphylaxis
5. Pollen grains

**B. Answer the following questions in brief.**

1. Write a note on food allergens.
2. How does strong sunlight act as an allergen?
3. Write the difference between allergy and allergen.
4. Write a note on different types of allergy.
5. List the precautionary measures to be taken against a pollen allergy.

**C. Answer the following questions in detail.**

1. Write a note on allergic reactions and their symptoms.
2. List different types of allergens and explain any two.
3. What are the precautionary measures to be taken against dust and food allergy?

### Application-based Question

Our immune system may be referred to as small bands of Japanese 'holdout' soldiers after World War II. Find out why.

### Picture-based Questions

Observe the images given below and answer the following questions.

1. What is the symptom shown in the first image?
2. What could be the possible allergen for the symptom shown in the first image?
3. What can cause the symptom shown in the second image?
4. List the possible food(s) that can cause the symptom shown in the second image?
5. Can moulds on the walls cause an allergic reaction? If yes, how?

a. 

b. 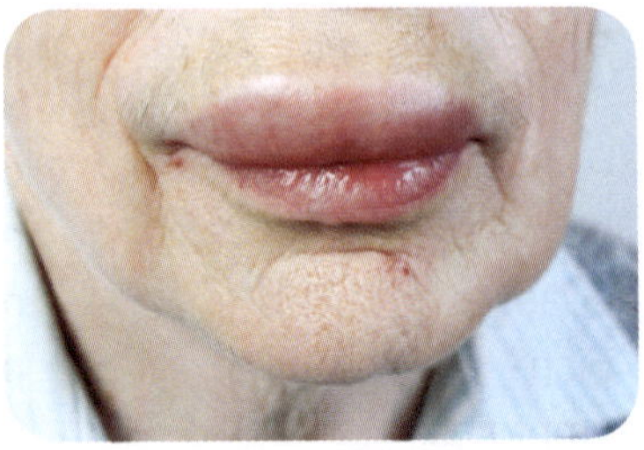

c. 

# Skill Booster

**A.** **21CS:** Critical Thinking | **EL** | **BT:** Psychomotor

Observe a permanent slide of pollen grains and dust mites that cause allergy. Draw your observations on a paper and use it for further reference.

**B.** **21CS:** Communication | **CC:** Health and Physical Education | **BT:** Affective, Psychomotor

Your school is celebrating an Allergy Awareness Week. Design your own poster. Write a catchy slogan beneath it. Paste your poster on the school notice board.

**C.** **21CS:** Critical Thinking | **CC:** Health and Physical Education | **BT:** Cognitive, Affective

Our health is affected by a variety of factors. Among these factors, our lifestyle plays a huge role in how healthy we are. From what we eat and drink, to how much we exercise, everything affects our health. Being aware of what is good for our health and what isn't help us make the right lifestyle choices.

List five healthy lifestyle choices that help keep you fit and protect you from diseases.

# Worksheet 6

Sam is a new boy in the school. Very few people in the class know him. One of his classmates offered him a cookie. Without asking for the ingredients in the cookie, Sam took a bite. Within a couple of minutes, he started to have difficulty in breathing and had to be rushed to the hospital. On admission to the hospital, it was revealed that he is allergic to one of the ingredients used in the cookie. He is lactose intolerant.

## My SEE Journal

A. Why was it essential to admit Sam to a hospital? What precautionary measure could he have taken to avoid this situation?

B. Are food allergy and food tolerance the same? Discuss and explain.

## My SDG Journal

3 GOOD HEALTH AND WELL-BEING

Around 30,000 food allergies are recorded for emergency treatments and 100 to 200 deaths per year are witnessed in the nation. Prepare an awareness poster and the precautions that can be taken to avoid the same.

# Review Corner

## Review 1 (Chapters 1–3) Maximum Marks: 40

**A. Choose the correct answer.** **(5 × 1 = 5)**

1. Kingdom, Phylum and Family are
   a. characteristics of an organism b. names of species
   c. taxonomical ranks d. different genera
2. Which of the following is a human parasite?
   a. Lobster b. Wasp c. Tapeworm d. Spider
3. Which of the following plant tissues conducts minerals and water?
   a. Parenchyma b. Phloem c. Collenchyma d. Xylem
4. Cells of which of the following tissues have a basement membrane?
   a. Nervous tissue b. Epithelial tissue c. Muscular tissue d. None of these
5. Which of these have organs called suckers?
   a. Oyster b. Slug c. Starfish d. Centipede

**B. Fill in the blanks.** **(5 × 1 = 5)**

1. Dendrons branch out to form ___________ (dendrites/axon).
2. False feet in *Amoeba* are also known as ___________ (pseudopodia/flagella).
3. Parrots have hollow bones, wings and ___________ (streamlined body/webbed feet) that help them fly.
4. Blood is a ___________ (fluid/fibrous) connective tissue.
5. ________ (Kingdom/Species) is the highest rank in taxonomy.

**C. Write T for True and F for False.** **(5 × 1 = 5)**

1. Smooth muscles are found in the internal organs of the body.
2. Aristotle gave the five-kingdom classification.
3. Newts belong to the class Reptilia.
4. Cells in the apical meristem divide actively.
5. Lateral meristem causes growth in length.

**D. Give reasons for the following.** **(5 × 2 = 10)**

1. Voluntary skeletal muscles work in pairs to bring about movement.
2. Plants stop growing when the apical meristem is removed.
3. Cardiac muscles do not get fatigued in the lifetime of an organism.
4. Sclerenchyma cells do not grow.
5. Adipose tissues insulate the body.

**E. Answer the following questions in brief.** **(5 × 3 = 15)**

1. Write a note on supporting tissues in plants.
2. What are the common characteristics of Platyhelminthes?
3. To which class of vertebrates do monkeys belong? Give the characteristic features of the class.
4. Explain the structure of stomata.
5. Write a note on skeletal tissues.

## Review 2 (Chapters 4–6)

**Maximum Marks: 40**

**A. Choose the correct answer.** **(5 × 1 = 5)**

1. Involuntary nervous system is also known as the
   a. autonomous nervous system b. somatic nervous system
   c. cranial nervous system d. spinal nervous system
2. Which of these is not a characteristic allergic reaction of hay fever?
   a. Red watery eyes b. Itchy and runny nose
   c. Scaly rashes on skin d. Continuous sneezing
3. Which of these is NOT a product of photosynthesis?
   a. Carbon dioxide b. Oxygen c. Water d. Glucose
4. How many molecules of carbon dioxide are formed at the end of anaerobic respiration?
   a. 2 molecules b. 4 molecules c. 6 molecules d. 8 molecules
5. Which of these factors does not affect the rate of photosynthesis?
   a. Light b. Water c. Oxygen d. Temperature

**B. Fill in the blanks.** **(5 × 1 = 5)**

1. The pores present in the leaves of plants are called ________ (guard cells/stomata).
2. In aerobic respiration, oxidation of glucose releases ________ (38 ATP/2 ATP) molecules.
3. The ________ (excretory/nervous) system helps in the control and coordination of the body.
4. Pollens are the ________ (female/male) gametes produced from the flowers.
5. ____________ (Stomata/Chlorophyll) absorbs sunlight and converts it into chemical energy.

**C. Write T for True and F for False.** **(5 × 1 = 5)**

1. A nerve cell is also called a nephron.
2. Asthma is characterized by difficulty in breathing.
3. Plants perform only photosynthesis during the daytime.
4. More energy is released during anaerobic respiration than during aerobic respiration.
5. Availability of water increases the rate of photosynthesis.

**D. Give reasons for the following.** **(5 × 2 = 10)**

1. The surface of cerebrum has many foldings called furrows and ridges.
2. Temperature above 30°C stops the process of photosynthesis.
3. Exposure of skin to strong sunlight may cause sun poisoning.
4. Muscle cells switch between aerobic and anaerobic respiration.
5. Plants need sunlight to prepare food.

**E. Answer the following questions in brief.** **(5 × 3 = 15)**

1. Write a short note on anaphylaxis.
2. Write a short note on urinary tract infection.
3. What is respiration? How do plants respire?
4. Explain the role of $CO_2$ as a factor affecting the process of photosynthesis.
5. Explain the structure of the human brain.

# STEAM Projects

## Observation of Microorganisms

Basic microscopes had already existed for almost half a century before Anton Van Leeuwenhoek started exploring microscopes. He was fascinated by the idea of being able to observe tiny creatures. He made simple microscopes using biconvex lenses that were capable of magnifying objects up to 200 times. In the 1670s, he observed bacteria under his own microscopes and was able to describe them. This was a significant improvement to the earlier microscopes developed by Zacharias Janssen in the 1590s.

Leeuwenhoek Microscope

Microscopes have been a tool of utmost importance in studying microorganisms. The current microscopes are highly advanced and can even observe neurons in the brain.

**Make a simple water microscope.**

**Things You Need**

1. A large paper clip
2. Pliers
3. Laser pointer
4. Adhesive tape
5. Pond water

**Let's Start:**

1. 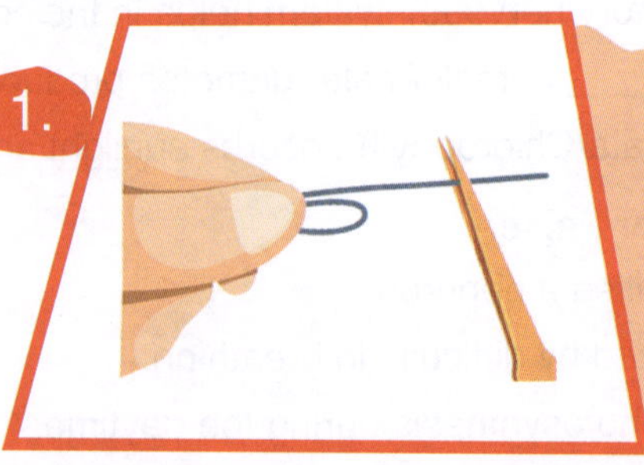

Using a plier, make the paper clip straight to make a wire.

2. 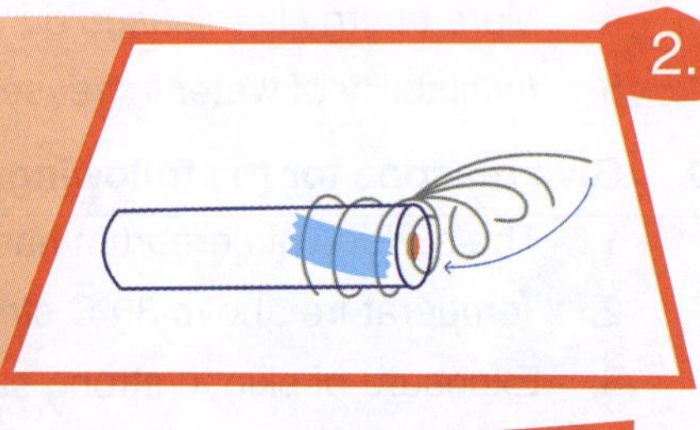

Wrap the paper clip wire around the laser pointer. Leave about 2 cm unwrapped at the front of the laser pointer. Tape the wire in place. Bend the unwrapped wire to make a loop in front of the laser pointer. Your simple microscope is ready.

3. 

Take a cup of pond water. Dip the wire loop of your microscope into the pond water.

4. 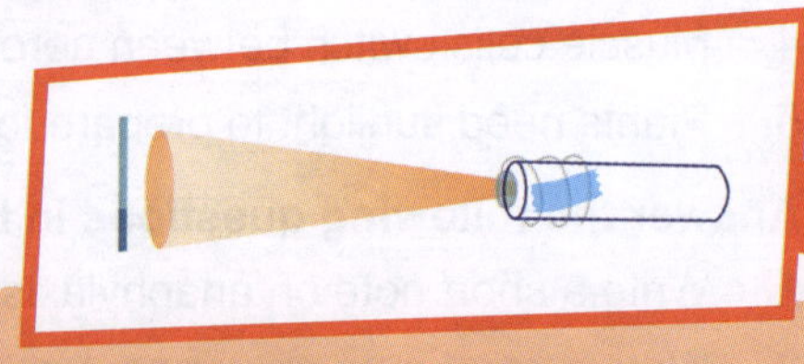

Turn on your laser pointer and point it towards a white surface. What do you see? (Make the room dark for better results!)

# Your Task

Microscopes are very versatile and are used in various fields of study, not just for observing microorganisms.
Find out about the different types of microscopes. What special purpose does each type of microscope provide?

One of the most advanced microscopes is the electron microscope. Write a note on the working of this microscope and the advantage it provides over other microscopes.

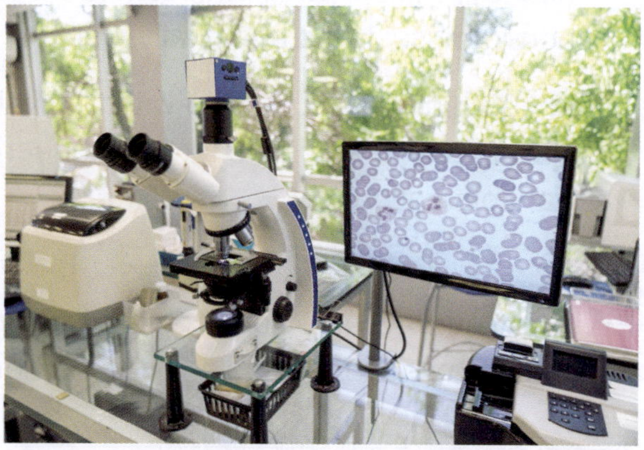

Most microscopes are expensive and are difficult to maintain. A lot of them cannot be moved around easily. The need for a portable microscope which can be used anywhere gave rise to Foldscope. It is an invention by Manu Prakash and Jim Cybulski. Foldscope is an inexpensive, highly portable microscope made of paper that gives a good magnification.
Procure a foldscope and observe any 3 things of interest around you and note down the observations.

# Role of Science in Benefitting the Society

## Organ Transplantation: One of the great advances in medical science

Dr Joseph Edward Murray was an American plastic surgeon. He spent most of his time caring for the casualties of the war. Working in the field of reconstructive surgery ignited his lifelong passion for correcting terrible physical deformities. He realized the profound impact a simple transplantation can have on a person's life. He had seen how the tissue of one person could be used to save the life of another.

He was the first surgeon to successfully perform organ (kidney) transplantation, first in identical twins, then in non-identical twins and finally, using a deceased donor.

In 1990, he was honoured with the Nobel Prize in Physiology or Medicine for his pioneering work in organ transplantation.

Dr Joseph Edward Murray
(1 April 1919–26 November 2012)

Who is your favourite science personality? Describe the personality's work and how he/she contributed to the society with his/her work.

_______________________________________________

_______________________________________________

_______________________________________________

_______________________________________________

_______________________________________________

Collect some pictures related to your favourite personality's work and paste in the space given below.